Around the World in a Salad Bowl

Around the World

IN

A Salad Bowl

BY VICTOR BENNETT

Collier Books, New York

Collier-Macmillan Ltd., London

First Collier Books Edition 1968

Published originally in hard cover by Hesperian House,
722 Montgomery Street, San Francisco 11

The Macmillan Company, New York
Collier-Macmillan Canada Ltd., Toronto, Ontario

Printed in the United States of America

CONTENTS

FOREWORD

By Alexander MacDonald

A long time devotee of the culinary magic of Victor Bennett, I was frankly skeptical of his ability to paddle himself around the storm-tossed seas of the world in something so small as a salad bowl! But a casual glance at the advance proofs of this book makes it certain in my mind that Victor, fresh from his voyagings, has come up with what I believe is the first and most important work yet published on the art of the tossed salad.

A combination of master chef and world traveler, Victor is perfect for the job. In Sydney, Australia, his periodic visits are awaited by the Down Under *cognoscenti* with a loosening of belts and a licking of lips. As far afield as Auckland and Hawaii he has left the unmistakable imprint of his chafing dish and salad bowl in the most patrician kitchens. His advice is sought after, his recipes guarded like first editions, and his memory hovers like a aura over some of the best banquet halls in the Western world. A graduate of the famed Chicago Pump Room, Seminar of the College Inn, past master of pyrotechnics at San Francisco's famed Top of the Mark, and most popular and combustible Maitre D' on the Matson Line's voyages in the South Pacific, Victor is the rarest of rare culinary creatures—the gourmet's gourmet; the chef of chefs; the expert to whom even fellow experts defer in matters pertaining to good things of the table.

The trouble with a Victor cookbook, however, is that I find it difficult to lay it down for months on end. He sent me his last opus—*Chafing Dish Magic*—and this resulted in my small entourage being expelled from our kitchen for six weeks, while the Young Master committed hari-kari nightly over the flame thrower, working his way through a succession of irresistible formulae (from which the only item lacking was the injunction "Take one young phoenix . . ."). For the cunning fiend set forth his repasts with such delicious persuasion that no sooner had I got Candied Chicken Livers (with brandy and cointreau) going like a house on fire than my roving eye caught a nearby come-hither for Chicken Breast Flambé (with apricot liqueur) and so, next night I was off again.

I once opened his first volume at random, saying confidently to myself, "This time I am beyond temptation, seeing that I am fresh out of Cognac, Cointreau, Benedictine, Chives and truffles, and have little in the larder but a hunk of cheese and nothing in the cellar beyond a few bottle of Chablis. . . ."

And what did I see on the first page I turned to? Why, a recipe for Welsh Rabbit, requiring nothing more than a few cups of grated cheese and a smitchin of white wine. . . .

I must confess that I was once a haphazard eater whose eyes were perpetually ablaze with indigestion. But a few short weeks with Victor—en route to San Francisco, aboard the S. S. *Mariposa*—fixed all that. He lectured me that a sauce can be something nobler than ketchup, that a salad is not for grazing but for eating, and that there are precisely three hundred and sixty five ways of cooking chicken.

In later months—after I committed the supreme folly of making a culinary crony of the man (with myself in the role of humble disciple) he proved a merciless taskmaster. Once he caught me using a garlic crusher—a device which expels the juice and pulp through needle-thin holes in its base. He explained that a garlic clove is not strangled like a mashed potato but chopped, coarse or fine as desired, with a sharp knife.

I shall never forget the look on his face when I confessed that I had been thickening my Sauce Robert with cornstarch. It was the infinitely reproachful gaze of Julius Caesar as he murmured "Et tu, Brute." "Alex," he said, slowly and somberly. "Let me tell you the Facts of Life. Cornstarch has its uses, and so has flour. Now, with flour, we make a *roux*, consisting of butter and. . . ."

I now make Sauce Robert with flour!

One night I found myself being ejected from the premises

of a Sydney nightclub for saying harsh words about a portion of Sargasso which the Maitre D'—a born *farceur*—described as an endive salad. Victor, who had been dining with me attempted to look the other way as we were escorted a bit unceremoniously through the portals. "Any idiot can make a salad!" I muttered as we reached the fresh air. Victor stopped short, and gazed at me with true distress. "Any idiot can make a salad!" he repeated, as though barely able to comprehend my blasphemy. Then, warming up in indignation, he continued, "Why, there are infinite varieties of salad. A man could write a *book* about the complexities of flavor and texture—the appearance—the—"

I cut him short. "Then why don't *you* write a book about it?" I suggested.

And he has. You have it in your hand. And bless me if the wizard of the wooden bowl hasn't actually transformed what to many is nothing but low calorie diet into the realm of high cuisine.

Let me remind readers of this book that salad-wise, we are living in a golden age. Only a few hundred years ago most of the fruits of the field were entered in the poisons book of the day. Robert Burton in his *Anatomy of Melancholy* stated:

Among herbs to be eaten I find gourds, cowcumbers, coleworts, melons disallowed, but especially cabbage. It causeth troublesome dreams, and sends up black vapors to the brain.

Some are of the opinion that all herbs and sallets breed melancholy, especially bugloss, borage and lettuce. Roots as garlick, onions, scallions, turnips, carrots and parsnips are windy, bad and troublesome to the head, as are all manner of fruits, as apples, plums, cherries and strawberries. They trouble the mind, and send gross fumes to the brain, making men mad. . . .

After those Dark Ages of the Dinner Table, along came Medical Science. And after Medical Science had given the green light to all these items (including bugloss and borage, to be sure) along came Victor Bennett to elevate the tossed salad and salad dressings into a culinary art. He has circumnavigated the globe to select only the best for the salad bowl. What follows is *your* voyage of salad discovery under the command of this Gilbertian figure, starting in San Francisco, which to me is the gourmet capital of the World.

YOUR GUIDE TO
THE PERFECT SALAD

BURNET: A delicate aromatic herb whose leaves are used for seasoning. According to Alexander Dumas, this plant was once highly esteemed as an astringent, a diuretic and for healing.

CABBAGE: The varieties of cabbage are legion, and most of them originate in Europe. In nearly every French province, cabbage is the staple of the farmers. Shredded with carrots and raisins, the humble cabbage provides an attractive salad for more leisured folk in the off-lettuce season.

CELERY: The ancients crowned themselves with celery at their feasts to neutralize the strength of wine. They called it *ache*. The Italian language took hold of this word and developed it into celery. To keep it from discoloring, place in a container or paper bag and store in a cool, dry place. Before serving in a salad, plunge celery sticks into ice-cold water to which a slice of lemon has been added.

CHAPON: According to Dumas, the idea of calling a crust of stale bread a chapon originated in Gascony. *The Dictionary of French Cooking* recommends the bread rubbed with garlic as a seasoning for chicory.

CHICORY: There are two sorts of chicory ideal for decorating salads: wild chicory and cultivated chicory (commonly known as endive). Wild chicory (dandelion), which is eaten only as young tender shoots, is also known by the somewhat Rabelaisian *pissabed*.

CHILLING: Immerse the torn lettuce in a large container or dishpan with salt water and at least two trays of ice cubes for 15 minutes. Remove lettuce and shake in a terry cloth towel. Lettuce and other salad greens will keep for several days if prepared by separating leaves and washing under running water. Allow to drain on paper towels. When almost dry, line a plastic sack with paper towels and lay greens on towels. Cover with more paper towels, close sack tightly, and refrigerate.

CUCUMBER: The cucumber appears in salads throughout the world. There is a theory that the peeled cucumber is more easily digested, but this has not been definitely established.

DRESSING: There are three basic salad dressings: the French, Mayonnaise and the Cooked Dressing. All others stem from these, and are simply variations. The basic French is made of olive oil, vinegar, salt and pepper. Mayonnaise is oil, vinegar, salt, pepper, mustard and raw egg. The ingredients are added slowly while the mixture is beaten. Cooked Dressings are a combination of sugar, salt, mustard, flour, egg, milk and vinegar cooked slowly over water with butter added.

EMULSIFY: To suspend an oil or fatty substance in a solution, as with oil and vinegar. Emulsification is achieved by beating the ingredients, sometimes with an egg beater.

ESCAROLE: A broad-leafed endive, with deep-green spiny leaves, the escarole is at its best in the chopped or tossed salad.

FENNEL: A very aromatic plant whose seeds have an odor of anise. Fennel is eaten like celery, especially in Central Italy where it is not unusual to come across people with a head of fennel under one arm, munching it with bread for lunch or dinner.

FRENCH ENDIVE: With slender fingers of crisp white, French endive belongs on an appetizer plate, or it may be served alone with a spicy dressing.

GARBANZOS: An Asiatic herb of the pea family, bearing short pods with pea-like seeds. Garbanzos is the Spanish word for chick peas.

GARLIC: The Egyptians worshiped it. The Greeks and the English detested it. The Romans ate it with delight. Modern Europeans as a whole use it sparingly. Not so in the United States where garlic flavors many salads—and many salad bowls. To perform this latter ritual, mash a garlic clove with salt, using a fork, against the wooden bowl. Repeat three or four times. Using a salad spoon on the mashed garlic, work into the wood in a circular motion. Alternatively, a chapon may be used, and the chapon may then be divided into cubes and tossed with the salad to which it imparts its flavor.

GARNITURE: Make sure that each salad served has the necessary eye appeal. Garniture is often a matter of individual taste and the host and hostess can extemporize on this theme with almost limitless variations.

LEEK: The national emblem of that tight little island, Wales, the leek originated in Spain. Europeans eat it raw with bread. It has a diuretic quality, and is used in French soups for flavoring. In Lorraine, according to Dumas, tarts are made with leeks.

LETTUCE: There are at least seven lettuces commonly marketed in the United States. The most widely used is the crisp, light green, tight-headed iceberg. The tenderest is the Boston "butter" lettuce. Another favorite is the Bibb. Other popular lettuces often used in mixed salads are escarole, romaine (sometimes called Cos), endive, chicory, watercress. Greens not as popular but used in season are: mustard greens (somewhat bitter), sharp young dandelions, tender young spinach, the individual Swiss chard, collards, rabb, celery cabbage, land cress, field salad and sorrel (sour grass).

MARINATE: To marinate is to marry. Allow ingredients to set together for a while in a solution (such as oil or vinegar) and you will achieve a perfect blend of flavors.

OLIVE OIL: To some palates, pure olive oil is too strong, too heavy. It can be lightened by mixing half and half with cold-pressed soybean oil or by adding high grade peanut oil or vegetable oil. Some gourmets prefer salads made with walnut oil.

PARSLEY: This is the obligatory condiment of every sauce. "Parsley," says the learned author of the *Traites Des Plantes Usuelles*, "makes food more helpful, more agreeable, it stimulates the appetite and helps digestion." Bosc is even more positive in his opinion. "Take parsley away from the cook, and you leave him in a situation where it is next to impossible for him to practice his art."

PARSNIPS: Not everyone likes the flavor of parsnips. The

English believe that when parsnips get too old they produce delirium and even madness.

PEPPER: Grind your pepper in a pepper mill as the salad is made. It should be freshly ground to be flavorsome.

READY TRAY: Before making the salad, organize the ingredients on a ready tray. Setting up the tray fixes the plan, the choice of salad, the ingredients, their measure, the order of their use. The ready tray cues the action and holds the secret knack of putting the salad together. Like the magician's prop table, it can make possible, too, the deft touch of showmanship.

SALAD BOWL: A large unfinished wooden salad bowl with wooden fork and spoon is the choice. After each use, rinse it with cold water: dry it with cloth toweling. This keeps the faint garlic flavor and in time the bowl will wear a fine patina. The wooden fork and spoon will not bruise the salad leaves. A second, ceramic, china, or glass bowl is also useful for salads without garlic, especially for fruit, or for fish salads. A smaller glass bowl is desirable, too, when mixing a single salad. On the shape, the deeper, the better. The deep bowl makes tossing easier and uses less dressing.

SHALLOTS: According to Dumas, shallots came from Syria to Europe with the homing Crusaders. Like onions and garlic, the shallot is used in sauces and salads, but it brings to them a quite distinctive flavor, much more delicate than the other two condiments named. Shallots are excellent in oil and vinegar sauces served with artichokes, hot or cold. It is impossible to make a really piquant sauce without shallots.

TARRAGON: An aromatic plant, originating in Siberia, much cultivated for seasoning of salads and to flavor vinegar.

TOMATO: The tomato is a native of Central and South America and was introduced into Spain by Cortez. From Spain it spread to Italy, suffered an eclipse, and was only rediscovered in the eighteenth century. Tomatoes add appetizing color, and can make a salad look beautiful in seconds.

SALADS AROUND THE WORLD

❧

San Francisco

HAWAIIAN FRUIT BOWL

(Serves 6)

- 1   Cup fresh orange sections
- 1   Cup fresh pineapple, diced into ½-inch cubes
- 1   Cup bananas, sliced ¼-inch thick
- 1   Cup seedless grapes
- 1   Cup mangos, diced into ½-inch cubes
- 1   Cup papaya, diced into ½-inch cubes
- 1   Cup miniature marshmallows
- 1   Cup fresh strawberries, halved
- ½   Cup fresh coconut, grated
- 1   Pint yogurt
-     Juice of 6 fresh limes
- 1   Large sprig of mint leaves, chopped fine
- ½   Cup Peppermint Schnapps liqueur
-     Lettuce leaves
-     Few whole strawberries for garnish

In a large wooden salad bowl place the fresh fruits, marshmallows and shredded fresh coconut.

In another bowl blend yogurt with lime juice and Peppermint Schnapps until smooth.

Add dressing to the fruit combination and mix gently.

Chill thoroughly until serving time.

Serve on lettuce leaves and add a few extra strawberries for garnish.

VICTOR ROMAINE SALAD

(Serves 4)

1 Clove garlic, peeled
1 Good-size wedge of Roquefort cheese
1 Fresh lemon (juice only, strained)
1 Tablespoon Sauce Diable by Escoffier (or substitute
      ½ tablespoon Worcestershire sauce and ½ table-
      spoon A-1 sauce)
½ Teaspoon dry mustard
3 Drops Tabasco sauce
1 Tablespoon pure olive oil
1 Cup sour cream
1 Head romaine lettuce, torn into bite-size pieces
   Paprika
   Salt, and pepper mill

Mash garlic pod with pinch of salt in wooden salad bowl
by placing the tongs of a dinner fork over the garlic pod and
bearing down. Repeat this three or four times, then take a
large-bowled salad spoon, placing the bowl of the spoon on
the mashed pieces of garlic, and move them in a circular
direction until the garlic juice is absorbed into the wood of
the bowl. This is referred to as flavoring the bowl.

Add the wedge of Roquefort cheese, lemon juice, Sauce
Diable, mustard, Tabasco, olive oil and sour cream. Mash,
blend and mix thoroughly with a flourish until a thick paste-
type dressing is accomplished.

Ladle amount of dressing desired over well-chilled romaine
in a wooden salad bowl; add pinch of paprika for eye-appeal,
salt and freshly ground black pepper to taste. Toss thoroughly
and serve on cold individual salad plates.

LOUIS LURIE SALAD

(*Serves 4 to 6*)

2   Heads romaine lettuce, torn into bite-size pieces
1   Cup celery, thinly sliced
6   Sprigs Italian parsley (clover type), chopped coarse
2   Large avocados, sliced in ¼-inch to ½-inch wedges
2   Medium-size tomatoes, sliced ¼-inch thick
6   Artichoke bottoms, pre-cooked
3   Quarter-inch slices Bermuda onion, separated into
    rings
4   Slices ¼-inch-thick fresh green bell pepper
2   Cups fresh cooked crabmeat, flaked
2   Cloves garlic
9   Tablespoons olive oil
3   Tablespoons tarragon white wine vinegar
1   Large lemon, squeezed, juice strained through nap-
    kin
    Salt, and pepper mill

Place lettuce in a large wooden salad bowl and sprinkle with celery and parsley. On the outer circumference lay the avocado alternated with tomato, then form the artichokes alternated with the onion rings as a garnish. Place on the center surface the green bell pepper rings and mount the flaked crab in their centers.

Prepare the dressing in a smaller wooden salad bowl by mashing garlic with the prongs of a dinner fork, adding enough salt to barely cover the garlic. Use the bowl of a wooden salad spoon to mash the garlic flavor into the surface of the wooden salad bowl. Add oil, vinegar, lemon juice, salt and freshly ground black pepper to taste. Mix well by rotating wooden salad fork in circular motion against surface of salad bowl in order to blend dressing and release garlic flavor into the dressing. When well-blended, pour over salad and toss thoroughly, but gently, so that each leaf is glistening and the garniture does not lose its eye-appeal by being broken into small pieces.

CRAB LOUIS

(Serves 2)

- 1   Good-size fresh crab, cooked and flaked (retain the whole legs)
- ½   Head lettuce, finely shredded
- 2   Hard-cooked eggs, chopped fine
- 1   Hard-cooked egg, sliced ¼-inch thick
- 2   Tablespoons chopped chives
- ½   Cup mayonnaise
- 2   Tablespoons olive oil
- 1   Tablespoon chili sauce
- 2   Tablespoons fresh green onions, finely chopped
- 1   Teaspoon horseradish
- 1   Teaspoon chopped pickle relish
- 1   Teaspoon Worcestershire sauce
- 1   Tablespoon tarragon wine vinegar
- 1   Tablespoon chopped pimento
- 1   Tablespoon chopped stuffed olives
    Salt, and pepper mill

On individual cold salad plates, place a mound of shredded lettuce; on the lettuce place a mound of the flaked crabmeat with whole pieces from the legs on top. Arrange a ring of the chopped eggs around the crab. Top with a few slices of hard-cooked egg and a sprinkling of chopped chives around the crab.

In a separate bowl blend thoroughly the mayonnaise, oil, chili sauce, onions, horseradish, relish, Worcestershire sauce, vinegar, pimento, olives and salt and freshly ground pepper to taste.

Serve the dressing separate from the salad.

GREEN GODDESS SALAD

(Serves 4)

- 1 Clove garlic, cut in half
- 2 Anchovy filets, cut fine
- 1 Tablespoon Bermuda onion, chopped fine
- 1 Teaspoon parsley, chopped fine
- 1 Teaspoon fresh tarragon leaves, chopped fine
- 1 Teaspoon chives, chopped fine
- 1 Teaspoon tarragon vinegar
- ¼ Cup mayonnaise
- 1 Head romaine, escarole or chicory, torn into bite-size pieces
   Pepper mill

Rub the inside of a wooden salad bowl with the cut side of the garlic. Add the anchovies, onion, parsley, tarragon, chives, vinegar and mayonnaise, and blend thoroughly.

Add salad greens, toss lightly and serve immediately on cold salad plates. Garnish with freshly ground black pepper to taste.

SALADS AROUND THE WORLD

❧

South Pacific

T A H I T I

~

SALAD "COUR DE COCOTIER" A LA TAHITIENNE

Millionaire's Salad
(Serves 4)

 1   Heart of coconut palm (canned or fresh)
 5   Green spring onions, thinly sliced
 ½   Teaspoon salt
 2   Tablespoons wine vinegar
 ¼   Teaspoon Worcestershire sauce
 2   Tablespoons tomato ketchup
 1   Teaspoon mustard
 3   Tablespoons pure olive oil (with or without a little
       dash of pressed fresh garlic)
     Few sprigs of fresh parsley, finely chopped

Slice coconut palm heart very thin.

Place in a wooden bowl; add the onions, salt, vinegar, Worcestershire sauce, ketchup, mustard and olive oil. Toss lightly.

Garnish with finely chopped parsley.

TAHITI

~

I'A OTA

Fish Salad
(Serves 4)

1 Raw fish, your choice, about 5 pounds
1 Cup fresh lime or fresh lemon juice
2 Bermuda onions, thinly sliced
6 Tablespoons olive oil
3 Tablespoons vinegar
Salt, and pepper mill

Bone the fish and cut it into pieces about 1-inch square and ½-inch thick. Put the pieces in a casserole and add the lime or lemon juice, leaving the fish to "cook" in this citric acid for approximately 1½ hours.

Drain off the juices and put the fish on a large platter with the onions.

Blend the olive oil, vinegar, salt and freshly ground black pepper to taste. Pour over the fish and onions. Toss lightly and serve on individual cold plates.

Another way to make a sauce is to grate a coconut (kernel) into its milk, squeeze through a cloth to extract the cream, add salt and white pepper to taste, thinly sliced raw onions and a little garlic.

The native name of the dish is *I'a Ota*. The fish is anything but raw, for it is completely cooked in the acid of the lime juice. It can also be used as an hors d'oeuvre. In Tahiti, it is widely known and appreciated as a specific for the man who has looked too long upon the flowing bowl the night before.

INDONESIA

❧

GADO-GADO

Mixed Salad
(Serves 6)

SALAD

½ Pound fresh cabbage, coarsely shredded
½ Pound fresh string beans, cut in 1-inch lengths
1 Pound fresh bean sprouts
1 Cucumber, medium size, unpeeled and sliced
1 Bunch radishes, sliced
2 Hard-cooked eggs, sliced for garnishing

Parboil cabbage, string beans and bean sprouts. Reserve cooking water. Cool thoroughly.

On individual cold salad plates equally arrange cooled vegetables, cucumber and radishes in layers. Garnish with slices of hard-cooked eggs. Serve with peanut-butter dressing and steamed wild rice.

DRESSING

1 Teaspoon salt
2 Teaspoons brown sugar
1 Teaspoon lemon juice
1 Teaspoon soya sauce
1 Bermuda onion, thinly sliced and sautéed lightly
2 Cloves garlic, chopped fine, sautéed lightly
1 Small hot red pepper, chopped fine
¼ Pound finely ground peanut butter
½ Cup warm water from boiled vegetables

Prepare the dressing in a bowl by crushing and mixing the ingredients and adding the warm vegetable water. Blend thoroughly.

13

A U S T R A L I A

~

AUSTRALIAN FRUIT SALAD

(*Serves 6 to 8*)

1 Small fresh pineapple, peeled and diced into ½-inch cubes
4 Bananas, peeled and diced
4 Tablespoons fresh lemon juice
4 Oranges, peeled, membrane removed, and diced
¼ Teaspoon salt
1 Apple, unpeeled and diced
1 Fresh pear, peeled and diced
2 Passion fruits, peeled and diced
4 Tablespoons powdered sugar
½ Cup whipping cream, whipped and sweetened
Sprigs of fresh mint

In a large salad bowl combine the pineapple and bananas, and sprinkle with lemon juice to minimize discoloration. Add oranges with juice and salt, apple, pear and passion fruits. Toss lightly and sprinkle with powdered sugar. Refrigerate for at least one hour.

Serve in sherbet glasses. Garnish with sweetened whipped cream and a sprig of fresh mint.

If passion fruit is unobtainable, papaya fruit may be substituted. Fresh, soft fruits in season such as peaches, small white grapes or very small melon balls may be added if desired, but pineapple, bananas, oranges and passion fruit are the essentials of the Australian-style fruit salad.

SALADS AROUND THE WORLD

India and the Far East

KOREA

~

SOOK CHOO NA MOOL

Bean Sprout Salad
(Serves 6)

¼ Cup salad oil
2 Tablespoons vinegar
2 Tablespoons soy sauce
½ Teaspoon salt
½ Teaspoon freshly ground black pepper
¼ Cup finely chopped scallions
¼ Cup thinly sliced pimento
2 Tablespoons ground sesame seeds
1 Garlic clove, finely chopped
2 Cups bean sprouts

In a small bowl blend together thoroughly the oil, vinegar, soy sauce, salt, pepper, scallions, pimento, sesame seeds and garlic.

Place the bean sprouts in a large wooden salad bowl.

Pour the dressing over the bean sprouts and toss gently.

Chill thoroughly for approximately one hour.

Serve on individual chilled salad plates.

JAPAN

~

JAPANESE SALAD

(Serves 6)

2 Pounds potatoes, peeled, boiled in beef broth
    Salt, and pepper mill
2 Tablespoons olive oil
1 Tablespoon vinegar
1 Cup white wine
1 Teaspoon fresh chervil, chopped fine
1 Teaspoon fresh chives, chopped fine
1 Teaspoon fresh tarragon, chopped fine
1 Shallot, chopped fine
1 Teaspoon parsley, chopped fine
1 Teaspoon fresh burnet, chopped fine
2 Dozen mussels, or very small clams
½ Cup water
1 Bermuda onion, medium size, chopped fine
2 Celery branches, coarsely cut
1 Teaspoon fresh mignonette, chopped fine
1 Teaspoon vinegar
1 Truffle, thinly sliced, cooked in champagne

Slice potatoes, while still warm, into a large salad bowl and season with salt and freshly ground black pepper to taste, olive oil, vinegar, wine, chervil, chives, tarragon, shallot, parsley and burnet. Toss gently but thoroughly and set aside.

In a large kettle cook mussels in one-half cup water with onion, celery, mignonette and vinegar, but no salt. Place over high heat, and toss frequently. When the shells open they are ready—take the mussel meat from the shells and cut away their foot or black appendage.

Add the mussels to the potatoes, toss lightly and cover the surface with truffles. Set the salad in a cold place for one hour and when serving, mix the truffles into the salad.

CHINA

ORIENTAL SALAD

(*Serves 4*)

½   Cup almonds, shredded
2½ Cups fresh peas, cooked and cooled
1   Cup cheddar cheese, cubed
1   Tablespoon pimento, finely chopped
¼   Cup dill pickle, chopped fine
⅓   Cup yogurt
½   Teaspoon prepared mustard
    Salt, and pepper mill
    Lettuce leaves

Combine the almonds, peas, cheese, pimento, pickle, yogurt and mustard in a salad bowl. Season to taste with salt and freshly ground black pepper. Toss gently. Chill.

Serve on lettuce leaves.

CHINA

~

CANTONESE SALAD

(Serves 6)

2	Cups fresh bean sprouts, thoroughly washed and dried
6	Tablespoons salad oil
2	Tablespoons vinegar
½	Teaspoon sugar
¼	Teaspoon paprika
¼	Teaspoon dry mustard
	Salt, and pepper mill
2	Cups cold cooked ham, cut in ½-inch cubes
1	Cup celery, thinly sliced
2	Tablespoons pimento, finely chopped
1½	Cups cold cooked kidney beans, drained
¼	Cup fresh green onions, finely chopped
2	Tablespoons green olives, chopped fine
	Dash of soy sauce
¼	Cup sour cream
	Crisp lettuce leaves

Place bean sprouts in a salad bowl.

Blend together thoroughly the oil, vinegar, sugar, paprika, mustard, salt and freshly ground black pepper to taste. Pour over the bean sprouts and marinate for several hours. Drain.

Add the ham, celery, pimento, beans, onions, olives, soy sauce and sour cream.

Toss lightly until well mixed.

Serve on crisp lettuce leaves.

C H I N A

~

CHINESE CABBAGE SALAD

(*Serves 4*)

- 1 Head Chinese cabbage, finely shredded
- 1 Fresh cucumber, unpeeled and diced
- 1 Green bell pepper, diced
- 1 Tablespoon Bermuda onion, chopped fine
- 1 Tablespoon sesame seeds, toasted
  Salt, and pepper mill
- ¼ Cup French dressing flavored with
- 1 Tablespoon soy sauce

In a wooden salad bowl combine cabbage, cucumber, green pepper, onion, toasted sesame seeds, salt and freshly ground black pepper to taste.

Add dressing and toss lightly.

Serve on individual cold salad plates.

CHINA

~

FAR EAST SALAD

(Serves 6)

½   Bunch curly endive, torn into bite-size pieces
1   Head romaine, medium size, torn into bite-size
        pieces
1   Cup Chinese cabbage, torn into bite-size pieces
⅔   Cup fresh pineapple, diced in ½-inch cubes
½   Cup celery, thinly sliced
1   Cucumber, medium size, peeled and thinly sliced
1   Raw carrot, medium size, thinly sliced
1   Cup cold cooked chicken, cut in ½-inch cubes
3   Tablespoons olive oil
1   Tablespoon wine vinegar
2   Tablespoons chutney, your choice
2   Hard-cooked eggs, finely chopped
½   Teaspoon curry powder
     Onion salt
     Freshly ground black pepper
     Dash of paprika
6   Lichee nuts, peeled, halved and pitted

In a large wooden salad bowl combine the endive, romaine, Chinese cabbage, pineapple, celery, cucumber, carrot and chicken.

In a smaller bowl, thoroughly blend the oil with the vinegar, chutney, eggs, curry powder, onion salt and freshly ground black pepper to taste. Add a dash of paprika for color.

Add dressing to the salad and toss lightly.

Sprinkle lichee nuts on top of salad.

Serve on individual chilled salad plates.

MALAYA

❧

SINGAPORE SALAD

(Serves 4)

SALAD
1 Quart bean sprouts
1 Pint boiling water
1 Avocado, peeled and thinly sliced in rings
1 Pimento, thinly sliced in strips

Pour boiling water over bean sprouts and discard any bruised pieces. Drain and chill.

Place a mound of chilled bean sprouts on individual chilled salad plates. Top with a chain of thin avocado rings and garnish with a small strip of pimento.

Delicately ladle just enough dressing over mound to insure juiciness, but not sogginess. Serve immediately.

DRESSING
1 Teaspoon dry mustard
1 Lemon (juice only)
1 Tablespoon tarragon vinegar
3 Tablespoons pure olive oil
   Salt, and pepper mill
   Pinch of sugar

Blend ingredients for dressing thoroughly and serve chilled.

THAILAND (SIAM)

~

YAM KOONG

Shrimp Salad
(Serves 6)

1   Cup fresh milk
1   Cup fresh coconut, grated
2   Pounds fresh raw shrimp, peeled and cleaned
2   Cups water
2   Teaspoons salt
1   Bay leaf
1   Tablespoon olive oil
2   Cloves garlic, chopped fine
2   Shallots, chopped fine
2   Green bell peppers, chopped fine
2   Tablespoons soy sauce
1   Raw apple, peeled and grated
3   Tablespoons chopped peanuts

Combine the milk and coconut in a saucepan. Bring to a boil, remove from the heat and let stand for 30 minutes. Press all the milk from the coconut, discard the pulp and set aside.

Combine the shrimp, water, salt and bay leaf in a saucepan. Boil for 8 minutes. Drain and split the shrimp lengthwise. Chill for 1 hour.

Heat the olive oil in a saucepan. Add the garlic and shallots and sauté for 2 minutes, stirring frequently. Remove from the heat. Add the green peppers, soy sauce, apple and peanuts. Toss thoroughly. Combine this mixture with the coconut milk and chill for at least 1 hour.

Arrange the shrimp on a platter; pour the dressing over them and serve cold from the platter.

BURMA

~

PRAWN SALAD

(*Serves 4*)

2 Pounds uncooked prawns
   Boiling salted water
½ Cup Bermuda onion, finely chopped
6 Limes (juice only)
   Salt, and pepper mill
   Crisp lettuce leaves
1 Teaspoon celery leaves, finely chopped
1 Teaspoon leek, finely chopped

Remove shells from prawns. With a sharp knife, cut down the length of each prawn and lift out the black vein. Drop prawns into boiling, salted water to cover, using 1 teaspoon salt to each quart of water. Reduce heat, cover and simmer to 10 minutes or until prawns are pink. Cool the cooked prawns thoroughly, then chop fine.

Combine finely chopped prawns, onion, lime juice, salt and freshly ground black pepper to taste. Toss lightly and chill.

Serve on crisp lettuce leaves and garnish with chopped celery leaves and leek.

INDIA

~

INDIA HOUSE SALAD

(*Serves 6*)

2	Heads romaine lettuce, torn into bite-size pieces
⅔	Cup peanut oil
1	Tablespoon Burgundy wine
1	Tablespoon garlic vinegar
1	Tablespoon red wine vinegar
½	Tablespoon tarragon vinegar
½	Tablespoon Worcestershire sauce
1	Teaspoon English dry mustard
1½	Teaspoons celery seeds
1	Teaspoon of curry powder
1	Clove garlic, chopped fine
	Salt, and pepper mill

Place the lettuce in a large wooden salad bowl.

Blend together thoroughly the peanut oil, Burgundy wine garlic vinegar, red wine vinegar, tarragon vinegar, Worcestershire sauce, mustard, celery seeds, curry powder, garlic salt and freshly ground black pepper to taste.

Pour over the romaine in the salad bowl and toss thoroughly, but gently, so as not to bruise the greens.

Serve immediately on cold salad plates.

INDIA

MAIWA KACHUMAR

Nut Salad
(Serves 4)

2   Cups chopped walnut meats
3   Dried figs, coarsely chopped
6   Dates, stoned and coarsely chopped
¼   Cup fresh coconut, shredded
2   Tablespoons raisins, washed and dried
1   Large apple, pared, cored and coarsely chopped
4   Sprigs watercress, chopped fine
1   Tablespoon melted butter
3   Tablespoons olive oil
1   Tablespoon wine vinegar
     Salt, and pepper mill
2   Fresh tomatoes, medium size, peeled and cut into
         wedges
     Crisp lettuce leaves

In a salad bowl combine the nuts, figs, dates, coconut,
raisins, apple, watercress and butter.
Blend the oil, vinegar, salt and freshly ground black pepper
to taste.
Add dressing to the salad and toss lightly.
Serve on crisp lettuce leaves and garnish with wedges of
tomato.

INDIA

~

INDIAN CABBAGE SALAD

(*Serves 4*)

- 2   Cups crisp cabbage, finely shredded
- ½   Cup cooked whole fresh kernel corn, cooled
- 2   Tablespoons green bell pepper, finely chopped
- 2   Tablespoons red sweet pepper, finely chopped
- ½   Tablespoon Bermuda onion, finely chopped
      Salt, and pepper mill
- 1   Teaspoon fresh chervil, finely chopped
- ⅓   Cup French dressing
      Crisp lettuce leaves

In a large salad bowl combine cabbage, corn, green pepper, red pepper, onion, salt, freshly ground black pepper to taste and chervil.

Add French dressing and toss lightly until well coated with the dressing.

Serve on crisp lettuce leaves on individual cold salad plates.

CEYLON

❧

ONION SAMBOL

(6 Small Servings)

1   Large Bermuda onion, finely sliced
1   Fresh cucumber, medium size, finely sliced
1   Green bell pepper, medium size, seeds removed and
        finely sliced
½   Fresh lemon (juice only)
     Salt, and pepper mill
3   Hard-cooked eggs, cut in half lengthwise

Combine onion, cucumber and green bell pepper in a
wooden bowl. Add lemon juice, salt and freshly ground black
pepper to taste. Toss lightly.

Garnish with eggs and chill thoroughly.

Serve as an accompaniment to curry and rice.

SALADS AROUND THE WORLD

❧

Africa and the Near East

A R A B I A

&

FATTOUSH

Mixed Salad
(Serves 6)

3 Fresh tomatoes, medium size, cubed
2 Fresh cucumbers, peeled and diced
1 Green bell pepper, chopped fine
8 Scallions, sliced thin
4 Tablespoons parsley, chopped fine
4 Sprigs fresh mint, chopped fine (or crème de
   menthe)
½ Cup olive oil
¼ Cup lemon juice
1 Teaspoon salt
2 Cups croutons

Combine and toss gently in a wooden salad bowl the tomatoes, cucumbers, green pepper, scallions, parsley and mint.

Blend the olive oil, lemon juice and salt together. Add to
the salad and toss lightly. Chill for 1 hour before serving.
Then add croutons, toss lightly and serve on cold salad plates.

Where fresh mint is not available a dash of crème de
menthe liqueur may be used. However, the liqueur should be
offered by the host or hostess to each guest.

PERSIA

~

PERSIAN CUCUMBER SALAD

(*Serves 2*)

1 Cucumber, peeled and thinly sliced
1 Garlic clove, chopped fine
½ Cup yogurt
   Salt, and pepper mill

Put cucumber slices on terry cloth or towel to drain.

Place cucumbers and garlic in porcelain bowl, cover and let stand for ½ hour.

Add yogurt and season to taste with salt and freshly ground black pepper.

Chill and serve.

AFRICA

CAPETOWN SALAD

(Serves 4)

- 2   Cups cold boiled African lobster tails, diced
- 2   Tablespoons sweet onion, chopped fine
- 1½ Cups celery, diced
- ¼ Cup French dressing
- ½ Cup sour cream
-    Salt, and pepper mill
- ⅛ Teaspoon paprika
-    Crisp romaine lettuce leaves
- 4   Lemon wedges or lime halves
- 4   Pimento strips

In a wooden salad bowl combine lobster, onion, celery and French dressing which has been blended with sour cream. Add salt, freshly ground black pepper to taste, and paprika.

Serve on crisp green romaine leaves with lemon wedges or lime halves. Garnish with pimento strips.

EGYPT

CUCUMBER AND YOGURT SALAD

(Serves 3)

½   Teaspoon fresh garlic, chopped fine
1   Teaspoon fresh mint, chopped fine
1   Cup yogurt
2   Cucumbers, medium size, unpeeled, thinly sliced
    Salt, and pepper mill
    Crisp green lettuce leaves
3   Radishes, medium size, thinly sliced

In a salad bowl thoroughly blend garlic and mint with yogurt.

Add cucumber slices and mix gently, but thoroughly. Season to taste with salt and freshly ground black pepper.

Serve on lettuce leaves and garnish with radish slices.

T U R K E Y

∽

JAJIK

Cucumber Salad
(Serves 6)

4 Cucumbers, peeled, quartered lengthwise and sliced
    fine
1 Teaspoon salt
1 Tablespoon distilled vinegar
1 Clove garlic, sliced thin
1 Teaspoon fresh dill, chopped fine
1 Cup yogurt
3 Tablespoons olive oil
1 Tablespoon chopped fresh mint leaves

Place cucumbers in a salad bowl and sprinkle with salt.
Put the vinegar and garlic in a cup and soak for 10 minutes.
Strain.

In a separate bowl place the dill and yogurt and add the
strained vinegar. Blend until smooth. Pour over the cucumbers and toss well. Sprinkle the olive oil and chopped mint
leaves on top of the salad.

Serve cool, but do not refrigerate.

TURKEY

SALAD CONSTANTINOPOLIS

(*Serves* 4)

4   Large red peppers
⅓   Pound fresh green beans
4   Fresh tomatoes, medium size
3   Anchovies, chopped fine
2   Cloves garlic, chopped fine
    Pepper mill
6   Tablespoons olive oil
3   Tablespoons wine vinegar

Bake peppers lightly in the oven, to dry the skin. Then peel off skin, remove seeds, slice thinly and place in bowl.

Boil green beans in salted water, drain and cool. Remove strings and cut in 1-inch pieces. Put in bowl with peppers.

Wash tomatoes, blanch and peel and remove seeds. Add to peppers and beans.

Add anchovies and garlic.

Season to taste with freshly ground black pepper.

Add oil and vinegar and toss gently.

Serve with any broiled or roasted meat.

Note: To remove seeds from blanched and peeled tomatoes cut in half and use tip of teaspoon.

Europe

F R A N C E

⌒

ORANGE AU BRULOT

Flaming Salad
(Serves 4)

4 Oranges, medium size
¾ Cup granulated sugar
½ Cup Jamaica rum, gently warmed

Peel oranges, remove white parts, quarter and place in
wooden salad bowl.
Sprinkle the sugar over the oranges and toss well.
Add rum to the oranges, set on fire and toss gently until
rum is completely burned out. The oranges will be syrupy.
Serve immediately on individual salad plates.
This salad is served in France during the Christmas and
New Year's holidays.

GREECE

~

GREEK SALAD

(*Serves 2*)

4 Lettuce leaves, crisp
1 Cup potato salad
1 Cup limestone lettuce, shredded
3 Sprigs watercress, finely chopped
1 Fresh tomato, peeled and quartered
1 Fresh cucumber, peeled, cut in half, sliced in quarters lengthwise
1 Slice feta cheese, cut in half
1 Green bell pepper, sliced in rings
1 Cooked beet, sliced thin
2 Scallions, sliced thin
1 Avocado, peeled, halved and sliced
6 Greek pickled peppers
4 Greek black olives
2 Boiled shrimp
2 Anchovy filets
1 Tablespoon tarragon vinegar
2 Tablespoons olive oil
¼ Teaspoon oregano
Salt, and pepper mill

Arrange crisp lettuce leaves on a platter and place potato salad in the center. Cover the potato salad with lettuce and watercress. Place tomato wedges around the potato salad mound. Stand the pieces of cucumber on end between the tomato wedges. Place cheese on top of the salad and decorate with rings of bell pepper and beet slices. Complete the decoration by placing the scallions and avocado slices vertically around the edge and border the platter with peppers and olives. Garnish the top with the shrimp and anchovy filets.

Sprinkle the salad with the dressing made of the vinegar, olice oil, oregano, salt and freshly ground black pepper to taste.

GREECE

∾

GREEK LETTUCE AND TOMATO SALAD

(*Serves 4*)

- 2 Fresh tomatoes, medium size, cut into wedges
- 1 Bermuda onion, medium size, thinly sliced
- 1 Tablespoon olive oil
  Salt, and pepper mill
- 1 Teaspoon fresh oregano, finely chopped
- 1 Clove of garlic, cut in half
- 1 Head lettuce, torn into bite-size pieces
- 1 Green bell pepper, seeds removed, and thinly sliced
- 1 Cucumber, medium size, unpeeled and thinly sliced
- 4 Radishes, thinly sliced
- 2 Stalks of celery, thinly sliced
- 2 Fresh green onions, thinly sliced
- 6 Tablespoons olive oil
- 3 Tablespoons tarragon wine vinegar
- ¼ Teaspoon dry mustard
  Juice of half lemon
  Salt, and pepper mill

Place tomatoes on plate and cover with thinly sliced onion. Allow to stand 10-15 minutes so tomatoes can absorb flavor of onion. Remove onion, sprinkle tomatoes with olive oil, salt and freshly ground black pepper to taste, and oregano. Set aside to use as garnish.

Rub the inside of a wooden salad bowl with the garlic.

Place the lettuce, green bell pepper, cucumber, radishes, celery and green onions in the salad bowl.

Blend the oil, vinegar, mustard, lemon juice, salt and freshly ground black pepper to taste.

Add dressing to the salad and toss gently.

Serve on individual cold salad plates and garnish with the tomatoes.

ITALY

∽

BREAD SALAD

(Serves 4)

1   Clove garlic
2   Fresh tomatoes, cut into wedges
1   Bermuda onion, medium size, thinly sliced
1   Teaspoon fresh basil, finely chopped
2   Cups Italian bread, cubed
     Salt, and pepper mill
3   Tablespoons olive oil
1½   Tablespoons wine vinegar

Rub the inside of a wooden salad bowl with the clove of garlic.

Place in the bowl and combine the tomatoes, onion, basil and bread. Season to taste with salt and freshly ground black pepper.

Thoroughly blend the oil and vinegar, add to the salad and toss the salad lightly.

Serve on chilled salad plates.

ITALY

∾

INSALATA DI CICORIA FINA

Dandelion Salad
(Serves 4)

1	Clove garlic
1	Pound dandelion greens, torn into bite-size pieces
12	Ripe black olives
4	Tablespoons olive oil
2	Tablespoons wine vinegar
	Salt, and pepper mill

Rub the inside of a wooden salad bowl with garlic.
Place the dandelion greens and olives in the bowl.
Pour olive oil and vinegar over leaves.
Season to taste with salt and freshly ground black pepper.
Toss thoroughly and serve on individual chilled salad plates
with garlic bread.

ITALY

INSALATA D'ESCAROLA

Escarole Salad
(Serves 4)

1   Head escarole, medium size, torn into bite-size piece
3   Tablespoons olive oil
1   Tablespoon tarragon vinegar
1   Teaspoon fresh sweet basil, finely chopped
     Salt, and pepper mill

Place escarole in a wooden salad bowl.

Blend the olive oil, vinegar, basil, salt and freshly groun
black pepper to taste.

Pour over salad and toss gently.

Serve on individual chilled salad plates.

ITALY

∽

INSALATA DI FAGIOLINI

String Bean Salad
(Serves 4)

1   Pound string beans, cut in half, cooked and cooled
4   Tablespoons olive oil
2   Tablespoons wine vinegar
1   Bermuda onion, thinly sliced
1   Clove garlic, finely chopped
1   Teaspoon fresh parsley, finely chopped
    Salt, and pepper mill
    Crisp lettuce leaves
1   Hard-cooked egg, chopped
    Parmesan cheese, grated

Place beans in a salad bowl.

Combine the olive oil, vinegar, onion, garlic, parsley, salt
and freshly ground black pepper to taste.

Pour over the beans and mix lightly. Cover and chill thoroughly in the refrigerator.

Serve on crisp lettuce leaves on individual salad plates and
sprinkle with egg and cheese.

ITALY

MAMA ROSSI'S SALAD

(*Serves 2*)

1 Cup butter lettuce, torn into bite-size pieces
6 Strips salami
6 Strips cheese, your choice
2 Anchovies, chopped
1 Tablespoon olive oil
1 Tablespoon wine vinegar
  Pinch of oregano
  Salt, and pepper mill
2 Slices Italian bread
2 Italian sausages, browned in wine

In a wooden salad bowl, toss lightly the lettuce, salami cheese and anchovies.

Blend the oil, vinegar, oregano and salt and freshly ground black pepper to taste. Pour over salad and toss lightly.

Serve in mounds over bread with sausages.

This is a good luncheon dish.

ITALY

~

INSALATA MISTA

Mixed Salad
(*Serves 6*)

1	Clove garlic
½	Head escarole, torn into bite-size pieces
½	Head chicory, torn into bite-size pieces
¼	Pound dandelion greens, torn into bite-size pieces
1	Cucumber, medium size, peeled and thinly sliced
6	Tablespoons olive oil
2	Tablespoons wine vinegar
	Salt, and pepper mill

Rub the inside of a wooden salad bowl with the garlic.

Add the greens and sliced cucumber.

Blend oil, vinegar, salt and freshly ground black pepper to taste and pour over the salad.

Toss lightly but thoroughly and serve immediately.

ITALY

❧

INSALATA DI PATATE E UOVA

Potato and Egg Salad
(Serves 6)

4 Large potatoes, boiled, cooled and diced
4 Hard-cooked eggs, quartered
½ Cup celery, thinly sliced
2 Teaspoons fresh parsley, finely chopped
6 Tablespoons olive oil
3 Tablespoons wine vinegar
Salt, and pepper mill

Combine potatoes, eggs, celery and parsley in a wooden salad bowl.

Blend oil with the vinegar and add to the salad.

Season to taste wtih salt and freshly ground black pepper.

Toss lightly and chill thoroughly in the refrigerator before serving.

ITALY

~

INSALATA DI LATTUGA ROMANA

Romaine Salad
(Serves 4)

1 Head romaine, torn into bite-size pieces
1 Large sweet onion, thinly sliced
3 Tablespoon olive oil
1 Tablespoon wine vinegar
  Salt, and pepper mill

In a wooden salad bowl, combine the romaine with the onion.

Blend oil, vinegar, salt and freshly ground black pepper to taste. Pour over salad.

Toss thoroughly, but gently, and serve immediately.

ITALY

~

INSALATA DI CALAMAI

Squid Salad
(Serves 4 to 6)

2 Pounds squid, cleaned and cut into 2-inch lengths
2 Cloves garlic, finely chopped
1 Tablespoon fresh mint, finely chopped
4 Tablespoons olive oil
  Juice of 1 large lemon
  Salt, and pepper mill
  Crisp lettuce leaves

Boil squid in 2 quarts of water about 30 minutes, or until tender. Drain well and cool thoroughly.

Blend the garlic with mint, olive oil, lemon juice, salt and freshly ground black pepper to taste.

Pour over squid in a salad bowl and toss lightly.

Serve on crisp lettuce leaves.

ITALY

❧

INSALATA DI FINOCCHIO, POMODORO E CICORIA

Fennel, Tomato and Chicory Salad
(Serves 6)

1 Clove garlic
1 Head fennel, thinly sliced
1 Head chicory, torn into bite-size pieces
2 Large fresh tomatoes, cut into wedges
   Salt, and pepper mill
6 Tablespoons olive oil
2 Tablespoons wine vinegar

Rub the inside of a large salad bowl with garlic.

Add fennel, chicory, tomatoes, salt and freshly ground black pepper to taste.

Blend the oil and vinegar. Pour over the salad.

Toss thoroughly and serve immediately.

S P A I N

~

REMOLACHA

Beet Salad
(Serves 4)

4   Beets, medium size
2   Cold boiled potatoes, thinly sliced
4   Whole green onions, thinly sliced
4   Sprigs parsley, finely chopped
3   Tablespoons olive oil
1   Tablespoon wine vinegar
    Salt, and pepper mill

Scrub beets clean. Bake in moderate oven (350° F.) until tender. Chill. Peel and cut into thin slices.

Place beets, potatoes, onions and parsley in a salad bowl.

Blend the oil, vinegar, salt and freshly ground black pepper to taste.

Pour the dressing over the salad and toss lightly.

Serve on chilled salad plates.

SPAIN

~

EGGPLANT SALAD

(Serves 6)

2 Eggplants, medium size, peeled and cut into 1-inch
   cubes
1 Teaspoon lemon juice
1 Teaspoon Bermuda onion, chopped fine
1 Cup celery, sliced fine
½ Cup chopped nuts
   Salt, and pepper mill
3 Tablespoons olive oil
1 Tablespoon wine vinegar
   Crisp romaine lettuce leaves
6 Hard-cooked eggs, quartered
   Spanish stuffed olives

Cook eggplants until tender in salted water to which the
lemon juice has been added. Drain and chill.

In a salad bowl mix the cooked eggplant with the onion,
celery, nuts, salt and freshly ground black pepper to taste.
Add olive oil and vinegar and toss gently.

Serve on romaine leaves and garnish with the eggs and
olives.

S P A I N

~

ENSALADA Á BILBAINITA

Codfish Salad
(*Serves 6*)

1　Smoked codfish
　　Milk
1　Head lettuce, torn into bite-size pieces
1　Head curly endive, torn into bite-size pieces
1　Green bell pepper, chopped
6　Spanish olives stuffed with almonds
2　Hard-cooked eggs, sliced
1　Clove garlic, gently crushed
6　Tablespoons Spanish olive oil
2　Tablespoons wine vinegar
4　Anchovies, rolled in oil, chopped fine
　　Pepper mill
　　Dash of cayenne
1　Pimento, sliced in thin strips for garnishing

Prepare codfish by soaking overnight in milk. Drain. Then simmer until tender in ½ cup of milk and ½ cup of water. Bone carefully, flake and chill.

In a large wooden salad bowl combine the codfish with the lettuce, endive, green pepper, olives and eggs.

Blend the garlic with the olive oil, vinegar, anchovies, freshly ground black pepper to taste and cayenne.

Add the dressing to the salad and toss lightly. Serve on individual cold salad plates. Garnish with pimento.

SPAIN

❧

ENSALADA DE ARROZ

Rice Salad
(Serves 6)

2   Cups rice, cooked and cooled
2   Green bell peppers, sliced fine
2   Pimentos, sliced fine
4   Fresh tomatoes, medium size, peeled and diced
2   Tablespoons Bermuda onion, chopped fine
2   Tablespoons parsley, chopped fine
¾   Cup olive oil
¼   Cup wine vinegar
    Salt, and pepper mill
1   Clove garlic, chopped fine
    Crisp lettuce leaves

In a salad bowl combine the rice, green peppers, pimentos, tomatoes, onion and parsley. Toss lightly with two forks.

Blend together the olive oil, vinegar, salt, freshly ground black pepper to taste and garlic. Pour over the rice in the salad bowl and again toss lightly.

Serve on crisp lettuce leaves on individual cold salad plates.

PORTUGAL

❧

SALADA DE PEPINO

(*Serves 6*)

1   Big red Spanish onion, thinly sliced
2   Big tart apples, peeled, cored and thinly sliced
1   Cucumber, medium size, unpeeled and thinly slice
2   Sweet green peppers, thinly sliced
2   Fresh ripe tomatoes, medium size, peeled and qua
      tered
1   Clove garlic, cut in half
½   Cup olive oil
¼   Cup fresh lime juice
      Salt, and pepper mill
6   Chestnuts
2   Hard-cooked eggs, chopped
6   Strips pimento

In a large wooden salad bowl combine the onion, apple
cucumber, peppers and tomatoes.

Rub a small wooden bowl with the garlic. Blend the oli
oil, lime juice, salt and freshly ground black pepper to taste.

Add the dressing to the salad and toss thoroughly. L
stand for about 1 hour.

Boil the chestnuts, peel and grate while piping hot. Coo
Sprinkle over the salad. Serve on cold salad plates.

Garnish with the eggs and pimento.

FRANCE

❧

SALAD NICOISE

(Serves 4)

2 Cups diced cold cooked potatoes
2 Cups cold cooked string beans, cut in 1-inch lengths
4 Anchovy filets, chopped fine
4 Black ripe olives, pitted and thinly sliced
1 Tablespoon capers
2 Tomatoes, medium size, quartered
1 Teaspoon fresh basil, chopped fine
3 Tablespoons olive oil
1 Tablespoon fresh lemon juice
Pepper mill

In a salad bowl combine the potatoes and beans.

Add the anchovies, olives, capers, tomatoes and basil and toss gently.

Blend the oil with the lemon juice and freshly ground black pepper to taste.

Add the dressing to the salad and toss lightly.

Serve immediately on chilled salad plates.

FRANCE

～

PARIS EXPOSITION, 1900
SALAD FRANÇILLON

(Serves 4)

1   Pound small potatoes, peeled and sliced
2   Cups consommé
3   Dozen small raw oysters
½   Pound truffles, washed, dried and thinly sliced
1   Cup sherry wine
1   Thick slice Bermuda onion
6   Tablespoons olive oil
3   Tablespoons wine vinegar
¼   Teaspoon paprika
       Salt, and pepper mill
¼   Glass champagne or Château Yquem, chilled, or
          California sweet white wine

Cook potatoes slowly in consommé for 20 minutes, or until tender, but not broken. Drain and refrigerate.

Parboil oysters. Drain and chill.

Cover truffles with sherry, add onion and cook for 5 minutes. Drain and allow to cool.

Arrange potatoes, oysters and truffles in a salad bowl and toss gently.

Blend the oil, vinegar, paprika, salt and freshly ground black pepper to taste with the champagne or wine.

Add dressing to the salad, toss gently and serve on chilled salad plates.

~

LETTUCE SALAD

(*Serves 6*)

2   Heads lettuce, torn into bite-size pieces
     Salt, and pepper mill
2   Fresh egg yolks
½   Cup fresh or sour cream
1   Dozen capers
4   Teaspoons tarragon vinegar

Place the lettuce in a large wooden bowl. Season to taste with salt and freshly ground black pepper.

Blend the egg yolks, cream, capers and vinegar until smooth.

Add the dressing to the lettuce in the salad bowl. Toss gently until every leaf is coated and glistening.

Sour cream may be substituted for fresh cream.

NANTES, FRANCE

∾

FISH AND ONION SALAD

(Serves 6)

   Butter
6 Small white onions, peeled and cored
6 Large sardines, boned, skinned and cut into ½-inch
     pieces
6 Hard-cooked eggs, sliced ½-inch thick
1 Teaspoon parsley, chopped fine
   Salt, and pepper mill
3 Tablespoons olive oil
1 Teaspoon fresh lemon juice
1 Teaspoon tarragon vinegar
6 Slices garlic cheese toast*
6 Sprigs parsley for garnishing

Put a little butter in the center of each onion and bake in a
covered pan for 1 hour or until tender. Cool, then slice.

In a salad bowl combine the onions, sardines, eggs, parsley,
and season to taste with salt and freshly ground black pepper.

Blend the olive oil, lemon juice and vinegar and add to the
salad. Toss gently. Refrigerate.

Serve on individual cold salad plates with garlic cheese
toast. Garnish with parsley.

* For recipe, see "How to Make Your Own."

FRANCE

∽

GASCONY SALAD

(Serves 4)

1 Large head curly endive, torn into bite-size pieces
1 Chapon* of French bread rubbed with garlic
2 Tablespoons olive oil
1 Tablespoon tarragon vinegar
  Salt, and pepper mill
3 Anchovies, cut into small pieces
½ Teaspoon celery seed

Place the endive in a wooden salad bowl with the chapon of French bread.

Thoroughly blend the olive oil, vinegar, salt, freshly ground black pepper to taste, anchovies and celery seed.

Add the dressing to the endive in the salad bowl and toss gently until the aroma from the chapon of French bread delicately permeates the air with the garlic fragrance.

Serve on individual cold salad plates.

* The end or heel of French bread; see "Your Guide to the Perfect Salad."

F R A N C E

~

CAPRICE SALAD

(*Serves 4*)

1 Head chilled butter lettuce, medium size, torn into bite-size pieces
4 Fresh ripe tomatoes, medium size, peeled and quartered
1 Cup fresh pineapple, julienned
1 Cup celery, thinly sliced
¼ Cup yogurt
1 Tablespoon whipped cream
1 Fresh lemon (juice only)
Dash of beet juice for color

In a wooden salad bowl combine lettuce, tomatoes, pineapple and celery.

Blend yogurt, whipped cream, lemon juice and beet juice. Add to salad and toss gently. Serve immediately.

FRANCE

ALEXANDER DUMAS' SALAD

(Serves 4)

1 Cup cold cooked potatoes, diced
1 Cup cold cooked beets, diced
1 Fresh tomato, medium size, peeled and diced
2 Tablespoons pickled gherkins, chopped fine
2 Anchovies, cut into small pieces
1 Tablespoon Bermuda onion, chopped fine
2 Hard-cooked eggs, quartered
1 Raw egg yolk, slightly beaten
1 Tablespoon olive oil
1 Teaspoon prepared mustard
  Salt, and pepper mill
  Crisp lettuce leaves

In a wooden salad bowl combine the potatoes with the beets, tomatoes, gherkins, anchovies, onion and eggs.

In a small bowl, blend until smooth the egg yolk with olive oil, mustard, salt and freshly ground black pepper to taste.

Add dressing to salad and toss lightly.

Serve on lettuce leaves on individual cold salad plates.

GERMANY

∽

HERRING SALAD

(Serves 2)

A traditional Christmas buffet specialty in German homes

1	10-ounce jar herring, drained and cut into ½-inch pieces
⅔	Cup cooked cold beets, coarsely chopped
1	Small Bermuda onion, thinly sliced
1	Small dill pickle, chopped fine
1	Tablespoon vinegar
¼	Cup sour cream
	Pepper mill

Combine the herring, beets, onion, and dill pickle in a salad bowl.

Blend the vinegar, sour cream and freshly ground black pepper to taste.

Add dressing to the salad bowl and toss gently but thoroughly.

Serve chilled on cold salad plates.

GERMANY

~

MAMA'S HOT POTATO SALAD

(*Serves* 6)

6	Medium-size hot boiled potatoes
1	Teaspoon sugar
¾	Teaspoon salt
¼	Teaspoon freshly ground black pepper
1	Small white onion, chopped very fine
4	Slices bacon, cut thin and chopped
¼	Cup cider vinegar, or enough to moisten potatoes
2	Hard-cooked eggs, chopped fine
1	Tablespoon parsley, chopped fine

Peel and slice potatoes while warm and keep them warm while preparing the dressing.

Place the potatoes in a large salad bowl, then add the sugar, salt, pepper and onion. Shake the potatoes so that the seasonings permeate them.

Place the bacon in a skillet and sauté over a slow fire until golden brown. Add vinegar to bacon and fat and cook until heated through. Pour mixture over potatoes, then add eggs and parsley. Shake and mix well.

Serve hot with warm boiled tongue, frankfurters or baked beans.

GERMANY

~

ASPARAGUS AND SHRIMP SALAD

(Serves 4)

1 Bunch asparagus, using only the tips, cut into
    1-inch pieces
1 Cup cooked shrimps, sliced
¼ Cup yogurt
1 Tablespoon capers
1 Teaspoon French mustard
    Salt, and pepper mill
    Lettuce leaves

Boil asparagus until tender. Drain and cool.

In a salad bowl combine the asparagus with the shrimps.

Blend the yogurt with the capers, mustard, salt and freshly
ground black pepper to taste.

Add the dressing to the salad and toss gently.

Serve on lettuce leaves on cold salad plates, with cheese and
crackers.

BULGARIA

~

MESHANA SALATA

Mixed Salad with Roast Peppers
(Serves 6)

4 Green bell peppers, washed and dried
3 Fresh tomatoes, medium size, sliced ¼-inch thick
2 Bermuda onions, medium size, sliced ¼-inch thick
2 Fresh cucumbers, unpeeled and sliced ¼-inch thick
3 Tablespoons vinegar
½ Cup olive oil
    Salt, and pepper mill

Place peppers on a fork, one at a time, and hold over a flame until the skin turns brown. Peel off the skin and cut the peppers into 1-inch strips. Chill for 1 hour.

Combine the peppers, tomatoes, onions and cucumbers in a salad bowl.

Blend the vinegar, oil, salt and freshly ground black pepper to taste and pour over the salad. Toss carefully and serve on individual cold salad plates.

POLAND

~

WARSAW SALAD

Mixed Salad
(Serves 8)

2 Cups cold cooked beets, diced
2 Cups cold cooked kidney beans, drained
2 Cups cold fresh cooked peas, drained
3 Dill pickles, chopped fine
3 Scallions, chopped fine
¾ Cup cold cooked crabmeat, flaked
½ Cup mayonnaise
1 Tablespoon prepared mustard
½ Cup sour cream
1 Hard-cooked egg, cut into strips
1 Raw carrot, medium size, cut into strips
8 Radishes for garnish
Salt, and pepper mill

In a salad bowl combine the beets, beans, peas, pickles, scallions and crabmeat.

Blend mayonnaise, mustard and sour cream until smooth. Pour over salad and toss lightly.

Season to taste with salt and freshly ground black pepper.

Serve on cold salad plates.

Garnish with egg, carrot and radishes.

HOLLAND

~

BISMARCK HERRING SALAD

(Serves 4)

1   Head butter lettuce, torn into bite-size pieces
1   Stalk celery, thinly sliced
2   Carrots, medium size, grated
1   Bismarck herring, thinly sliced
3   Tablespoons olive oil
1   Tablespoon fresh lemon juice
2   Tablespoons prepared chili sauce
   Pepper mill

In a wooden salad bowl combine lettuce, celery, carrots and herring.

Blend the oil, lemon juice and chili sauce until smooth.

Add dressing to ingredients in the salad bowl and toss lightly until thoroughly mixed.

Serve on individual cold salad places and garnish with freshly ground black pepper to taste.

S W I T Z E R L A N D

⌒

GRUYÈRE CHEESE SALAD

(*Serves 2*)

½ Pound Gruyère cheese, cut into ½-inch cubes
2 Tablespoons olive oil
1 Tablespoon wine vinegar
2 Bermuda onions, medium size, sliced very thin
2 Teaspoons dry mustard
   Salt, and pepper mill
   Crisp lettuce leaves

In a salad bowl toss thoroughly the cheese with olive oil, vinegar, onions, mustard, salt and freshly ground black pepper to taste.

Marinate for several hours before serving.

Serve on crisp lettuce leaves.

NORWAY

SALMON SALAD

(Serves 3)

1 Pound cold cooked salmon, skinned, boned and
  flaked
3 Hard-cooked egg yolks, sliced
1 Tablespoon ripe olives, chopped fine
1 Tablespoon capers
1 Tablespoon gherkin pickles, chopped fine and flaked
  Salt, and pepper mill
2 Tablespoons mayonnaise
  Lettuce leaves
1 Cup aspic jelly, refrigerated and diced into ¼-inch
  cubes

In a salad bowl combine the salmon with the egg yolks,
ves, capers, pickles, salt, freshly ground black pepper to
ste and mayonnaise.

Toss lightly and serve on lettuce leaves on cold salad plates.
Garnish with aspic jelly.

S W E D E N

~

SWEDISH SALAD

(Serves 4)

4 Sardines, boned, skinned and each cut into 4 piec
½ Cup cold beef or pork roast, cut into 1-inch cubes
1 Teaspoon onion juice
1 Beet, cooked and sliced
1 Potato, cooked and diced
1 Teaspoon parsley, chopped fine
6 Tablespoons olive oil
2 Tablespoons tarragon vinegar
   Salt, and pepper mill
   Crisp lettuce leaves
2 Hard-cooked eggs, quartered

In a salad bowl combine the sardines, meat, onion jui
beet, potato and parsley.

Blend the oil, vinegar, salt and freshly ground black pepp
to taste.

Add the dressing to the salad and toss gently.

Serve on lettuce leaves and garnish with the eggs.

S W E D E N

~

SWEDISH POTATO SALAD

(*Serves 6*)

1   Cup cold sliced cooked potatoes
2   Cooked beets cut in 1-inch strips
1   Head lettuce, torn into bite-size pieces
2   Tablespoons drained capers
2   Raw egg yolks, beaten smooth
½   Teaspoon salt
½   Teaspoon dry mustard
1   Teaspoon sugar
3   Tablespoons oil
1   Tablespoon vinegar
1   Tablespoon caper liquid
¼   Cup heavy fresh cream

Combine potatoes, beets, lettuce and capers in a salad bowl.

Blend together until smooth the egg yolks, salt, mustard and sugar. Gradually add the oil, vinegar and caper liquid. Add cream and blend until smooth.

Pour dressing over salad and toss lightly.

Serve on chilled salad plates.

For low calorie diet, substitute yogurt instead of heavy cream.

DENMARK

~

POTATO SALAD

(Serves 4)

1 Bermuda onion, medium size, thinly sliced
¼ Cup butter
3 Tablespoons vinegar
  Salt, and pepper mill
1 Pound potatoes, boiled, peeled and sliced
1 Teaspoon chives, chopped fine
1 Teaspoon parsley, chopped fine

Sauté onion lightly in butter, add vinegar, salt, and freshly ground black pepper to taste.

Gently add sliced potatoes. Heat them thoroughly without browning, being careful not to mash them.

Sprinkle with chives and parsley and serve immediately.

DENMARK

~

HUMMER SALAT

Danish Lobster Salad
(Serves 2)

1 Cup cooked cold lobster meat, flaked
½ Cup fresh-cooked cold asparagus tips, cut into
    ½-inch lengths
    Salt, and pepper mill
¼ Cup sour cream
2 Crisp lettuce leaves
2 Slices pumpernickel bread, buttered
4 Asparagus tips for garnish

In a salad bowl mix lobster, asparagus, salt and freshly
ground black pepper to taste with sour cream.
Place lettuce leaf on bread and mount with lobster salad.
Garnish with asparagus tips.

DENMARK

~

FISK SALAT

Danish Fish Salad
(Serves 6)

2   Cups cold boiled salmon, cod or halibut, cut into
    ½-inch cubes
1   Celery heart, boiled, chilled and cut into 1-inch
    pieces
1   Cup sliced cooked mushrooms, chilled
4   Tablespoons butter
¼   Cup flour
1½ Cups fish stock
1   Teaspoon salt
½   Teaspoon freshly ground black pepper
1   Tablespoon vinegar
½   Teaspoon sugar
3   Raw egg yolks, beaten smooth
1   Tablespoon sherry wine
1   Tablespoon fresh parsley, chopped fine
    Crisp lettuce leaves

In a wooden salad bowl combine fish, celery and mushrooms.

Melt butter in saucepan. Blend in flour and stir until smooth. Gradually add fish stock and cook until thick. Add salt and pepper.

Remove from heat and cool slightly. Add vinegar, sugar, egg yolks, wine and parsley. Blend until smooth.

Add dressing to salad and toss lightly.

Serve on crisp lettuce leaves.

FINLAND

∾

FINNISH SALAD

(*Serves 4*)

- 1 Cup cooked cold beef or ham, cut in thin strips
- ½ Cup raw apple, unpeeled and diced
- ½ Cup cooked carrots, cooled and diced
- 1 Cup cooked fresh peas, cooled
  Salt, and pepper mill
- 2 Tablespoons sour cream
- ¼ Cup whipping cream, whipped stiff
- ½ Fresh lemon (juice only) or
  Equivalent amount of sweet pickle juice

In a salad bowl combine meat, apple, carrots and peas. Season to taste with salt and freshly ground black pepper.

Thoroughly blend sour cream, whipping cream and lemon juice. Add to salad and toss lightly. Serve on individual cold salad plates.

FINLAND

～

SILLISALAATI

Herring Salad
(*Serves 6*)

1	Salt herring
1	Cup cooked beets, cooled and diced
1	Cup cooked carrots, cooled and diced
1	Cup cooked potatoes, cooled and diced
1	Cup fresh apple, diced
½	Cucumber, peeled and diced
1	Fresh tomato, medium size, diced
2	Small Bermuda onions, chopped fine
	Lettuce leaves
	Pepper mill
1	Cup sour cream
¼	Cup vinegar
	A little beet juice for coloring

Soak salt herring in cold water to partially freshen. Do n‹ cook. Remove skin and bone, cut herring into small piec‹ and place in a salad bowl. Add beets, carrots, potatoes, appl‹ cucumber, tomato and onions. Toss gently until thorough‹ mixed.

Serve on lettuce leaves on individual cold salad plates. Ga‹ nish with freshly ground black pepper.

Combine sour cream, vinegar and beet juice, but do n‹ mix this dressing with the salad. Serve it separately.

This also may be served for smorgasbord, in which case ‹ will serve 12.

RUSSIA

～

MEATLESS RUSSIAN SALAD

(*Serves 4*)

3 Raw carrots, medium size, coarsely grated
3 Fresh ripe tomatoes, medium size, thickly sliced
1 Bermuda onion, medium size, thinly sliced
1 Bunch watercress, stems removed and using only
  the leaves
  Salt, and pepper mill
½ Cup sour cream
  Crisp lettuce leaves
2 Tablespoons capers

In a salad bowl combine the carrots with the tomatoes,
nion, watercress, salt and freshly ground black pepper to
aste. Add sour cream and toss lightly.
Serve on lettuce leaves and garnish with capers.

RUSSIA

ROUSSKI SALAD

Russian Salad
(*Serves 6*)

1 Cup meat, game, poultry, or fish, cooked and diced or uncooked herring cut in small pieces
1 Cup beets, cooked and diced
1 Cup potatoes, cooked and diced
½ Cup gherkins, chopped fine
½ Cup salt cucumber or fresh cucumber, coarsely chopped
4 Hard-cooked eggs, chopped coarsely
½ Cup black olives, pitted
1 Cup fresh sauerkraut, drained and chopped
1 Cup cooked kidney beans, drained and rinsed with cold water
4 Tablespoons olive oil
4 Tablespoons cider vinegar
1 Teaspoon dry mustard
  Salt, and pepper mill
  Crisp lettuce leaves

Russian salad is often confused with a macédoine or mixture of small cut vegetables and cooked mixed vegetables with a mayonnaise dressing. The real Russian salad contains not only cooked vegetables, but also cooked meat, poultry, cooked fish, or uncooked herrings and it usually is dressed with plain dressing of oil, vinegar, salt and pepper; hence the name Vinaigrette, by which it is known in Russia.

Gently but thoroughly combine the meat, beets, potatoes, gherkins, cucumbers, eggs, olives, sauerkraut and beans in salad bowl.

Blend the oil, vinegar, mustard, salt and freshly ground black pepper to taste.

Add dressing to the salad bowl and toss lightly.

RUSSIA

∽

RUSSIAN GOLD SALAD

(Serves 8)

6	Hard-cooked eggs, chopped fine
1	Bermuda onion, medium size, chopped fine
6	Tablespoons melted butter
1	Teaspoon salt
½	Teaspoon freshly ground black pepper
1	4-ounce jar red carviar
1	Cup sour cream

Combine the eggs, onion, butter, salt and freshly ground black pepper in a salad bowl.

Blend the caviar and sour cream. Add to the salad bowl and toss gently.

Chill thoroughly before serving.

Serve on individual salad plates.

RUSSIA

~

RUSSIAN MIXED SALAD

(*Serves 6*)

9 Lettuce leaves
1 Cup cold cooked chicken, diced
1 Cup cold cooked tongue, diced
1 Cup cold cooked fish, diced, sturgeon preferred
2 Carrots, cooked and diced
4 Potatoes, medium size, cooked and diced
1 Cup string beans, cooked and cut in 1-inch pieces
6 Tablespoons olive oil
2 Tablespoons cider vinegar
  Salt, and pepper mill
⅔ Cup sour cream

On a lettuce-covered platter, arrange the chicken, tongue and fish in three parts, with the tongue in the center. Border with the carrots, potatoes and string beans, being careful to keep each vegetable distinct.

In a small bowl, thoroughly blend the olive oil, vinegar salt and freshly ground black pepper to taste. Pour over the salad.

Serve sour cream in a separate dish so that it can be offered to the guests.

RUSSIA

❧

SLADKY PEREZS

Sweet Pepper Salad
(Serves 6 to 8)

8 Green bell peppers, quartered, after removing seeds
    and fibers
2 Cups water
2 Teaspoons prepared mustard
2 Teaspoons sugar
1 Teaspoon salt
2 Tablespoons vinegar
½ Cup olive oil

Place peppers in a saucepan with the water. Boil for 20
minutes or until tender. Drain and cool in the refrigerator for
1 hour.

Combine the mustard, sugar, salt, vinegar and oil in a bowl
and blend thoroughly. Pour over the peppers.

Marinate for 2 hours. Serve very cold.

ENGLAND

~

YORKSHIRE SALAD

(Serves 6)

3 Tablespoons molasses
6 Tablespoons vinegar
½ Teaspoon freshly ground black pepper
2 Heads crisp lettuce, shredded
3 Scallions or fresh green onions, finely sliced
Salt

Combine the molasses, vinegar and pepper in a small bowl and blend thoroughly.

In a wooden salad bowl combine the lettuce and scallions. Add the dressing from the small bowl and toss until the lettuce is well coated. Season to taste with salt.

Serve cool, but not ice-cold.

ENGLAND

~

SALMAGUNDI

Herring-Chicken Salad
(*Brought to England from Spain*)
(*Serves 4*)

2 Large Dutch or Scotch herrings, washed, boned and
  flaked
1 Cup cold cooked white meat of chicken, diced
2 Hard-cooked eggs, sliced
1 Bermuda onion, chopped fine
1 Anchovy, chopped fine
1 Tablespoon ham or tongue, chopped fine
2 Tablespoons olive oil
1 Tablespoon vinegar
  Salt, and pepper mill
  Lettuce leaves

In a salad bowl combine the herrings with the white meat
of chicken, eggs, onion, anchovy and ham or tongue.

Blend the oil with the vinegar, salt and freshly ground black
pepper to taste.

Pour the dressing over the salad and toss lightly.

Serve on lettuce leaves on cold individual salad plates.

WALES

~

NEW LEEK SALAD

(*Serves 4*)

1 Chapon* of French bread rubbed well with garlic
1 Head chilled romaine lettuce, torn into bite-size pieces
3 Leeks, using the white young and tender parts, cut up coarsely
1 Large fresh tomato, cut into eighths
1 Teaspoon fresh sweet basil, finely chopped
1 Teaspoon fresh chervil, finely chopped
1 Tablespoon olive oil
2 Tablespoons cider vinegar
  Salt, and pepper mill

Put chapon in wooden salad bowl and add romaine, then the leeks and tomato and sprinkle with sweet basil and chervil. Toss lightly.

Blend the olive oil, vinegar, salt and freshly ground black pepper to taste. Add to the salad. Toss until romaine leaves are well coated.

Serve on cold salad plates.

* The end or heel of French bread; see "Your Guide to the Perfect Salad."

CZECHOSLOVAKIA

⁓

POTATO AND SAUERKRAUT SALAD

(Serves 6)

   6 Potatoes, boiled
   1 Cup sauerkraut, finely chopped
   3 Tablespoons oil
   ½ Teaspoon caraway seeds
   1 Tablespoon vinegar
     Sugar
     Salt

Peel and slice the cooked potatoes while still hot and place in a wooden salad bowl.

Add the sauerkraut and toss gently.

In a small bowl, blend the oil, caraway seeds, vinegar, sugar and salt to taste. Add to the potatoes and sauerkraut and toss gently so that the slices of potatoes remain whole.

Serve immediately.

SALADS AROUND THE WORLD

Latin America

GUATEMALA

ENSALADA DE GUACAMOLE

Avocado Salad
(Serves 4)

2   Avocados, peeled and diced
2   Hard-cooked eggs, diced
3   Small fresh tomatoes, peeled and diced
6   Stuffed Spanish olives, sliced
1   Small Bermuda onion, finely chopped
1   Small fresh chili pepper, finely chopped
    Salt, and pepper mill
    French dressing
    Crisp green lettuce leaves
4   Slices bacon, fried until crisp

In a salad bowl combine avocados, eggs, tomatoes, olives,
onion and chili pepper.

Season to taste with salt and freshly ground black pepper.
Add enough French dressing to moisten and toss gently.

Serve on lettuce leaves with slices of crisp bacon.

MEXICO

~

MEXICAN GUACAMOLE
CAULIFLOWER

(Serves 4)

1 Head cauliflower, medium size
   Crisp lettuce leaves
6 Tablespoons olive oil
3 Tablespoons eschalot wine vinegar
   Salt, and pepper mill
1 Bermuda onion, medium size, chopped fine
2 Avocados, medium size, mashed with wooden spoon
2 Fresh firm ripe tomatoes, peeled and diced
1 Teaspoon salt

Cook whole cauliflower in salted water until tender but do not over-cook. Chill thoroughly.

Arrange lettuce leaves on platter and place chilled cauliflower on them.

Blend oil, vinegar, salt and freshly ground black pepper to taste and pour over the cauliflower.

Blend together into a paste the onion, avocados, tomatoes and salt. Frost cauliflower evenly with this mixture. Serve chilled. Cut into individual portions.

MEXICO

༄

MEXICAN CABBAGE SALAD

(Serves 4)

- 1 Green bell pepper, chopped
- 3 Fresh green onions, thinly sliced
- 2 Cups cabbage, finely shredded
- ½ Cup yogurt
  Salt, and pepper mill
  Leaf lettuce leaves
- 2 Fresh tomatoes, medium size, peeled and sliced
  ¼-inch thick
- 1 Cucumber, unpeeled, scored and sliced ¼-inch
  thick

In a large wooden salad bowl combine the green pepper, onions, cabbage and yogurt. Season to taste with salt and freshly ground black pepper.

Toss lightly and serve on lettuce on individual salad plates. Garnish with tomato and cucumber slices.

MEXICO

⁓

GUACAMOLE

Avocado Salad
(Serves 4)

1 Small Bermuda onion, chopped fine
1 Fresh tomato, peeled, chopped fine
2 Large avocados, peeled and mashed with wooden
    spoon
2 Teaspoons chili powder
1 Teaspoon salt
2 Teaspoons vinegar
   Crisp green lettuce leaves

Combine the onion, tomato and avocados in a salad bowl.
Add the chili powder, salt and vinegar. Toss lightly until well
blended.

Serve on lettuce leaves.

CHILE

✧

ENSALADA CAMPESINA

Peasant Salad
(Serves 4)

1   Cup dried chick peas (garbanzos)
½   Pound Monterey Jack cheese, diced
2   Bermuda onions, medium size, thinly sliced
½   Cup olive oil
¼   Cup fresh lemon juice
1   Teaspoon salt
½   Teaspoon ground coriander
    Crisp lettuce leaves
3   Hard-cooked eggs, quartered

Soak the chick peas overnight in water to cover. Drain well. Add fresh water and cook for 2 hours or until tender. Drain well and chill thoroughly.

Combine the chick peas, cheese and onions in a salad bowl.

Blend the olive oil, lemon juice, salt and coriander together. Pour over ingredients in salad bowl and toss lightly.

Serve on lettuce leaves and garnish with the eggs.

CHILE

∾

BOCADO PRIMAVERA DE AVE

Chicken and Corn Salad
(Serves 6)

3   Cups cold boiled chicken, diced
2   Cups cooked cold fresh corn kernels
6   Fresh tomatoes, medium size, diced
3   Green bell peppers, finely chopped
½   Cup mayonnaise
    Salt, and pepper mill
    Crisp green lettuce leaves
3   Hard-cooked eggs, quartered
6   Radish roses
6   Ripe olives

In a large wooden salad bowl combine the chicken, corn, tomatoes, green peppers, mayonnaise, salt and freshly ground black pepper to taste. Toss gently, but thoroughly.

Serve on lettuce leaves on individual cold salad plates and garnish with eggs, radishes and olives.

JAMAICA

∽

IRIS SALAD

(*Serves 6*)

DRESSING

1   Clove garlic, chopped fine
¼   Cup wine vinegar
¼   Teaspoon salt
⅛   Teaspoon freshly ground black pepper
     Dash of paprika
¾   Cup olive oil
1   Tablespoon green bell pepper, chopped fine
1   Tablespoon pimento, chopped fine
1   Tablespoon green olives, chopped fine
1   Tablespoon sweet pickles, chopped fine

Place the garlic in the vinegar and allow to remain for 30 minutes. Strain, discarding the garlic. Combine thoroughly the salt, pepper, paprika, oil and vinegar in a bowl. Add the green pepper, pimento, olives and pickles. Blend well and chill thoroughly before serving.

SALAD

2   Heads romaine lettuce, washed and dried
       thoroughly
3   Fresh tomatoes, peeled and sliced ½-inch thick
3   Hard-cooked eggs, sliced
¼   Cup chopped blanched almonds
2   Bananas, diced

Arrange the romaine leaves on individual cold salad plates. Place 2 slices of tomato on each plate and place egg slices on the tomatoes. Sprinkle some almonds on each. Add the diced bananas to each portion. Pour the salad dressing over each salad and serve.

99

SALADS AROUND THE WORLD

The United States
and Canada

UNITED STATES

༄

ANCHOVY SALAD

(Serves 4)

6 Anchovies, cut into small pieces
3 Heads limestone* lettuce, torn into bite-size pieces
2 Hard-cooked eggs, chopped coarsely
1 Tablespoon chives, chopped fine
1 Teaspoon fresh fennel, chopped fine
4 Tablespoons sour cream
   Pepper mill

In a wooden salad bowl combine the anchovies with the
lettuce, eggs, chives, fennel and sour cream.
Season to taste with freshly ground black pepper.
Toss lightly and serve on chilled salad plates.

* If limestone is not available, butter lettuce may be used.

BACON SALAD

(Serves 6)

8 Slices bacon, diced, fried crisp and drained
2 Heads romaine lettuce, torn into bite-size pieces
2 Fresh tomatoes, cut in small wedges
½ Cup Romano cheese, grated
6 Fresh green onions, chopped fine
½ Teaspoon fresh mint, chopped fine
½ Teaspoon fresh oregano, chopped fine
⅓ Cup olive oil
3 Tablespoons fresh lemon juice
   Salt, and pepper mill
1 Clove garlic, chopped fine
1 Fresh whole raw egg, beaten lightly
1 Cup croutons, toasted until crisp

In a large wooden salad bowl combine the bacon with the romaine, tomatoes, cheese and onions.

In a small bowl, blend thoroughly the mint with oregano, oil, lemon juice, salt, freshly ground black pepper to taste and garlic. Add egg and blend until smooth.

Add dressing to the greens and toss thoroughly.

Add croutons and serve immediately on chilled salad plate.

BARBECUE SALAD

(*Serves 8*)

8	Slices bacon, diced
1½	Tablespoons flour
1	Cup white wine
½	Cup cider vinegar
	Salt, and pepper mill
½	Teaspoon fresh ginger, sliced fine
½	Teaspoon fresh thyme, chopped fine
½	Teaspoon fresh basil, chopped fine
6	Potatoes, medium size, boiled, cooled and sliced
1	Fresh cucumber, unpeeled and sliced ¼-inch thick
2	Stalks celery, sliced ¼-inch thick
2	Large Bermuda onions, thinly sliced in rings
1	Small head romaine, torn into bite-size pieces
½	Cup ripe olives, pitted and chopped fine
1	Kosher dill pickle, chopped fine
½	Cup fresh string beans, cut in inch length, cooked, cooled and drained
½	Cup fresh Chinese peas, cooked, cooled and drained
	Lettuce leaves
	Radish roses

Fry bacon until crisp. Drain off drippings. Measure ¼ cup drippings and mix with bacon in pan. Add flour, then gradually blend in wine vinegar, salt and freshly ground black pepper to taste, ginger, thyme and basil. Cook slowly until thick, stirring constantly.

In a small bowl, combine the potatoes, cucumber, celery, onions, romaine, olives, pickle, green beans and peas.

Spoon vegetables into the frying pan. Toss lightly until the vegetables are coated with the dressing.

Serve on lettuce-lined salad plates and garnish with radish roses.

BROCCOLI SALAD

(Serves 4)

- 2 Cups fresh broccoli, parboiled and chilled
- 1 Cup fresh ripe tomatoes, cut in small wedges
- 1 Cup celery, thinly sliced
- 1 Small Bermuda onion, chopped fine
- 1 Teaspoon fresh basil, chopped fine
  Salt, and pepper mill
- 2 Tablespoons olive oil
- 1 Tablespoon garlic wine vinegar
- 1 Teaspoon horseradish
  Lettuce leaves

In a salad bowl combine the broccoli, tomatoes, celery
onion, basil, salt and freshly ground black pepper to taste.

In a smaller bowl, blend until smooth the oil, vinegar an
horseradish.

Add dressing to the salad, toss lightly and serve immedi
ately on lettuce leaves on cold salad plates.

BRUSSELS SPROUTS SALAD

(*Serves 4*)

2 Cups fresh brussels sprouts, boiled until tender,
     drained and cooled
1 Bermuda onion, medium size, thinly sliced in rings
4 Ripe pitted olives, chopped fine
1 Tablespoon walnut meats, chopped fine
1 Tablespoon capers
2 Tablespoons fresh lemon juice
     Salt, and pepper mill
2 Tablespoons sour cream
     Lettuce leaves
     Paprika

In a wooden salad bowl, combine the sprouts with the
onion, olives, nut meats, capers and lemon juice.
Season to taste with salt and freshly ground black pepper.
Add sour cream and toss gently.
Serve on lettuce leaves on cold salad plates. Garnish with
paprika.

CABBAGE SALAD

Cole Slaw
(Serves 4)

1 Head firm cabbage, finely shredded and chopped
  Salt, and pepper mill
2 Fresh raw whole eggs
2 Tablespoons sugar
1 Tablespoon melted butter
1 Teaspoon prepared mustard
½ Cup cider vinegar
½ Cup sour cream

Put the cabbage in a wooden salad bowl and season to t
with salt and freshly ground black pepper.

In a saucepan beat the eggs with the sugar, butter, mus
and vinegar. Set over a low flame and cook until mix
thickens, stirring to keep it from sticking to the bottom of
pan. Remove from fire and add sour cream. Cool thoroug

Add the dressing to the cabbage and toss thoroughly.

Serve immediately.

CABBAGE SALAD,
SOUTHERN STYLE

(Serves 6 to 8)

4 Cups firm cabbage, finely shredded
1 Cup raw cauliflower, coarsely chopped
1 Cup celery, chopped fine
1 Cup sour cream
¼ Cup mayonnaise
1 Tablespoon tarragon vinegar
  Salt, and pepper mill
1 Tablespoon sugar
¼ Cup fresh green onions, chopped fine
¼ Cup green bell pepper, chopped fine
½ Cup cucumber, unpeeled, chopped fine
1 Tablespoon butter
½ Cup salted peanuts, coarsely chopped
2 Tablespoons grated Parmesan cheese

In a wooden salad bowl toss together the cabbage, cauliflower and celery.

In a small bowl, blend the sour cream with mayonnaise, vinegar, salt and freshly ground black pepper to taste, sugar, onions, bell pepper and cucumber. Set aside.

Melt butter in a small skillet, add peanuts and sauté until lightly browned. Remove from heat and immediately stir in the cheese.

Add dressing to the salad and toss lightly.

Serve on individual cold salad plates. Garnish the top of each with the sautéed peanuts.

CAESAR SALAD

(Serves 2)

2	Garlic cloves, peeled
8	Croutons, ¾-inch cubes, well-toasted and rubbed well with garlic
8	Anchovy filets
1	Fresh whole egg, coddled
1	Whole lemon
½	Teaspoon dry mustard
1	Tablespoon Worcestershire sauce
1	Tablespoon wine vinegar
4	Tablespoons olive oil
3	Drops Tabasco sauce
4	Tablespoons Parmesan cheese, grated
1	Head romaine, iceberg or butter lettuce
1	Teaspoon freshly ground black pepper

Use large wooden bowl that is very dry. Place garlic in bowl and mash by forcing the garlic through the prongs of a fork. Cover mashed garlic delicately with salt. Now force the garlic fibers and juice into the wood, using the bowl of a large metal spoon. The salt will help to scratch and force out the garlic fibers. Use a forcing, pressing, rotary movement. Add several croutons to bowl, mixing these around delicately in a circular movement to capture the garlic flavor in surface of bowl, then set croutons aside for use later.

Add 6 anchovy filets and mince. Add coddled egg. Squeeze lemon, strain through napkin to hold back pulp and seeds, and add with dry mustard, Worcestershire sauce, vinegar, olive oil and Tabasco sauce. Sprinkle 3 tablespoons of the cheese on the surface of the dressing and using a fork, whip it into a good consistency. Add torn greens, making sure they are well chilled, with water shaken off. Toss well but do not bruise the greens. Sprinkle with desired amount of freshly ground black pepper and toss again.

Sprinkle remaining tablespoon of cheese on surface of salad and toss again until every green leaf glistens with the dressing. To prevent sogginess, add garlic-flavored croutons at last moment. Serve on well-chilled salad plates, adding two anchovy filets in a criss-cross "X" design.

For lunch or a torrid mid-noon snack, this is a real taste treat when served with cheese or garlic toast* plus a favorite beer.

* See "How to Make Your Own."

CELERY SALAD

(*Serves 6*)

Dash of salt
1 Clove garlic, cut in half
1 Head leaf lettuce, torn into bite-size pieces
1 Cucumber, medium size, peeled and thinly sliced
1 Cup celery, thinly sliced
3 Hard-cooked eggs, quartered
2 Fresh tomatoes, medium size, peeled and quartered
½ Cup cooked ham, julienned
½ Cup cooked turkey, julienned
½ Teaspoon dry mustard
½ Teaspoon salt
1 Teaspoon Bermuda onion, chopped fine
2 Tablespoons vinegar
6 Tablespoons salad oil
1 Teaspoon celery seeds
Salt, and pepper mill
Sprigs of fresh watercress for garnish

Sprinkle a little salt over a large wooden salad bowl, then rub the cut clove of garlic over the bowl.

In the salad bowl combine the lettuce, cucumber, celery, eggs, tomatoes, ham and turkey.

In a smaller bowl combine the mustard, salt, onion and half of the vinegar and blend until smooth. Gradually add the oil, stirring constantly. Add the remaining vinegar and the celery seeds and blend until smooth.

Add the dressing to the salad. Toss gently until the dressing is well blended with the ingredients. Season to taste with salt and freshly ground black pepper.

Serve on cold salad plates and garnish with fresh watercress.

CHEF'S SALAD BOWL

Western Style
(Serves 4)

1   Clove garlic, peeled
1   Head romaine or your favorite lettuce, torn into
        bite-size pieces
1   Cup cold cooked ham, cut into ¼-inch wide strips
¼   Pound Swiss cheese, cut into strips ¼-inch wide
¼   Pound American cheese, cut into strips ¼-inch wide
1½ Pounds white asparagus tips, pre-cooked, drained
        and chilled
½   Cup cooked garbanzo beans, chilled
4   Radishes, medium size, sliced
2   Hard-cooked eggs, cooled and sliced
2   Tablespoons honey
1   Teaspoon horseradish
1   Teaspoon salt
1   Teaspoon dry mustard blended with wine vinegar
        until smooth
1   Teaspoon paprika
⅓   Cup herb vinegar
3   Tablespoons lemon juice
1   Tablespoon grated Bermuda onion
¼   Cup vegetable oil
    Salt, and pepper mill

Rub the inside of a wooden bowl with the garlic. Add the lettuce, ham, cheeses, asparagus tips, garbanzo beans, radishes and eggs. Toss lightly.

In a small bowl blend thoroughly the honey, horseradish, salt, mustard, paprika, vinegar, lemon juice, onion and oil.

Pour dressing over the salad and toss gently. Add salt and freshly ground pepper to taste.

CHICKEN-AVOCADO SALAD

(Serves 4)

½   Cup cooked cold chicken, diced into ½-inch cubes
1   Avocado, peeled, diced into ½-inch cubes
1   Head limestone lettuce, torn into bite-size pieces
2   Tablespoons crumbled Roquefort cheese
1   Tablespoon fresh lemon juice
3   Tablespoons sour cream
1   Teaspoon dry mustard
1   Garlic clove, chopped fine
   Salt, and pepper mill

Combine the chicken, avocado and romaine in a salad bowl

Blend the cheese with the lemon juice until smooth. Add the sour cream, mustard, garlic and salt and freshly ground black pepper to taste. Blend thoroughly.

Add dressing to salad in the bowl and toss gently.

Serve on cold salad plates and garnish with a dash of freshly ground black pepper.

CHICKEN LIVERS SALAD

(*Serves 4*)

½   Pound fresh chicken livers
¼   Cup butter
1   Head Bibb lettuce, torn into bite-size pieces
½   Bunch curly endive, torn into bite-size pieces
4   Fresh green onions, thinly sliced
¼   Cup crumbled Roquefort cheese
2   Hard-cooked eggs, chopped coarsely
½   Teaspoon dry mustard
3   Tablespoons olive oil
1   Tablespoon wine vinegar
½   Clove garlic, chopped fine
1   Teaspoon capers
    Salt, and pepper mill

Sauté the chicken livers in the butter until lightly browned. Chill thoroughly. Cut into bite-size pieces.

In a large wooden salad bowl, combine the chicken livers, lettuce, endive, onions, cheese and eggs.

In a smaller bowl blend together until smooth the mustard, oil, vinegar, garlic, capers, salt and freshly ground black pepper to taste.

Add dressing to the salad and toss gently.

Serve on individual cold salad plates.

CURLY ENDIVE SALAD

(Serves 6)

1 Clove garlic, peeled and cut in half
1 Head curly endive, torn into bite-size pieces
2 Cups potatoes, boiled, cooled and sliced
4 Hard-cooked eggs, quartered lengthwise
¼ Cup olive oil
  Juice of 2 fresh lemons
1 Teaspoon fresh oregano, finely chopped
  Salt, and pepper mill

Rub the inside of a wooden salad bowl with the garlic.

Add the endive, potatoes and eggs to the bowl.

Blend the olive oil, lemon juice and oregano. Pour this dressing over the salad and toss lightly.

Season to taste with salt and freshly ground black pepper, toss lightly and serve immediately on chilled salad plates.

EGG SALAD

(Serves 4)

8   Hard-cooked eggs, quartered
2   Cups lettuce, torn into bite-size pieces
½   Cup celery, thinly sliced
8   Anchovy filets, cut into small pieces
3   Tablespoons salad soil
1   Tablespoon vinegar
¼   Teaspoon sugar
¼   Teaspoon paprika
¼   Teaspoon dry mustard
    Pepper mill
    Lettuce leaves

In a wooden salad bowl toss together the eggs, lettuce, celery and anchovies.
Blend together until smooth the oil, vinegar, sugar, paprika, mustard and freshly ground black pepper to taste.
Add the dressing to the salad and toss lightly.
Serve on crisp lettuce leaves on cold salad plates.

ESCAROLE SALAD

(*Serves 6*)

- 1 Head escarole, torn into bite-size pieces
- ½ Bunch watercress, leaves only, stems removed
- ⅓ Cup radishes, sliced thin
- ½ Cup celery, sliced thin
- 1 Cup fresh uncooked green string beans, French cut
- 1 Cup cold cooked ham, julienned
  Salt, and pepper mill
- 3 Ounces bleu cheese
- 3 Tablespoons wine vinegar
  Dash of steak sauce
- ½ Cup olive oil
- 1 Clove garlic, crushed gently

In a large wooden salad bowl combine escarole, watercress, radishes, celery, green beans and ham.

Season to taste with salt and freshly ground black pepper.

In a smaller bowl, blend the cheese, vinegar, steak sauce, olive oil and garlic until smooth. Remove garlic before adding the dressing to the salad.

Add dressing to the salad and toss lightly.

Serve immediately on cold salad plates.

FENNEL SALAD

(*Serves 4*)

1   Large head of fennel
¼   Cup olive oil
2   Tablespoons red wine vinegar
      Salt, and pepper mill

Trim tops from the fennel, leaving heart intact; wash thor-
ughly. Cut in ½-inch pieces.
Blend the oil, vinegar, salt and freshly ground black pepper
 taste.
Pour the dressing over the fennel and toss lightly.
Serve immediately.

FENNEL-LETTUCE SALAD

(*Serves 4 to 6*)

1   Head Bibb lettuce, torn into bite-size pieces
1   Head romaine lettuce, torn into bite-size pieces
1   Small head curly endive, torn into bite-size pieces
1   Fennel heart, thinly sliced
½   Cup radishes, thinly sliced
4   Anchovies, cut into small pieces
4   Tablespoons olive oil
2   Tablespoons fresh lemon juice
½   Teaspoon dry mustard
¼   Teaspoon paprika
½   Small white onion, finely chopped

In a large wooden salad bowl combine the lettuce, romaine,
dive, fennel and radishes.
In a smaller bowl, blend the anchovies, olive oil, lemon
ce, mustard, paprika and onion together until smooth.
Pour dressing over the salad in the bowl and toss lightly, but
roughly, until the dressing has permeated the greens.
Serve on individual cold salad plates.

FRESH FRUIT AND
LETTUCE SALAD

(Serves 6)

- 1   Cup fresh pineapple, cut into 1-inch cubes
- 1   Fresh pear, peeled, cut into 1-inch cubes
- 1   Large red apple, unpeeled, cored and cut into ½-inch cubes
- 1   Head butter lettuce, torn into bite-size pieces
- 1   Cup celery, thinly sliced
- 2   Tablespoons butter
- 1   Teaspoon flour
- 3   Tablespoons cider vinegar
- 3   Tablespoons sherry wine
- 1   Tablespoon granulated sugar
- ½   Teaspoon prepared mustard
     Salt, and pepper mill

In a large wooden salad bowl combine the pineapple, pear, apple, lettuce and celery.

Melt butter in small saucepan.

Stir in flour.

Combine vinegar, wine, sugar, mustard, salt and fresh ground black pepper to taste.

Stir into butter-flour mixture. Simmer until thickened, stirring constantly. Cool, but do not chill.

Add dressing to the salad and toss gently, but thoroughly Serve on cold salad plates immediately.

GRAPEFRUIT SALAD

(*Serves 4*)

1 Small head lettuce, torn into bite-size pieces
1 Large grapefruit, peeled and shredded coarsely
2 Tablespoons olive oil
1 Tablespoon fresh lemon juice
  Salt, and pepper mill
  Paprika

Combine the lettuce with the grapefruit in a wooden salad
bowl.

In a small bowl, blend the olive oil, lemon juice, salt and
freshly ground black pepper to taste with enough paprika for
a good color.

Add the dressing to the salad and toss thoroughly.

Serve immediately on cold salad plates.

GREEN PEPPER SALAD

(*Serves 4*)

6 Green bell peppers, free from seeds, thinly sliced
1 Large Bermuda onion, thinly sliced
  Salt, and pepper mill
1 Teaspoon prepared mustard
½ Cup olive oil
  Juice of 1 large fresh lemon
1 Inch preserved ginger, cut fine
  Crisp lettuce leaves

In a wooden salad bowl combine the peppers with onion.
Season to taste with salt and freshly ground black pepper.
Blend thoroughly the mustard, olive oil, lemon juice and
ginger.

Add dressing to the salad and toss lightly.

Serve on crisp lettuce leaves.

GREEN SALAD

(*Serves 4*)

1   Bunch raw spinach, stems removed and leaves torn
     into bite-size pieces

½   Bunch curly endive, torn into bite-size pieces

1   Small head leaf lettuce, torn into bite-size pieces

⅓   Cup green olives, pitted and sliced

3   Fresh green onions, sliced fine

3   Tablespoons olive oil

1   Tablespoon wine vinegar
     Salt, and pepper mill

2   Fresh tomatoes, medium size, cut in wedges

In a large wooden salad bowl combine the spinach, endive
and lettuce.

Add the olives, onions, olive oil, vinegar, salt and freshly
ground black pepper to taste and toss lightly.

Serve on cold salad plates and garnish with tomato wedges.

GREEN SALAD SUPREME

(*Serves 6*)

- 1   Head Boston lettuce, torn into bite-size pieces
- ½   Head escarole, torn into bite-size pieces
- ½   Bunch watercress, stems removed from the leaves
- ½   Bunch curly endive, torn into bite-size pieces
- ½   Bunch fresh spinach leaves, torn into bite-size pieces
- 2   Teaspoons chives, chopped fine
- 1   Teaspoon sugar
- ½   Teaspoon celery seeds
- ½   Teaspoon dry mustard
- 2   Tablespoons wine vinegar
- 6   Tablespoons olive oil
      Salt, and pepper mill

In a large wooden salad bowl combine the lettuce, escarole, watercress, endive, spinach and chives.

Combine the sugar, celery seeds and mustard.

Add the vinegar and blend thoroughly.

Slowly add the oil, beating constantly.

Season to taste with salt and freshly ground black pepper.

Add dressing to salad and toss thoroughly.

Serve on cold salad plates.

KIDNEY BEAN SALAD

(Serves 4)

- 2 Cups red kidney beans, cooked and rinsed in cold water
- ½ Pound sausage, sautéed lightly
- ½ Cup celery, thinly sliced
- 3 Sweet pickles, coarsely chopped
- 1 Fresh tomato, peeled and diced
- 1 Bermuda onion, medium size, finely chopped
- 1 Hard-cooked egg, coarsely chopped
- 2 Tablespoons fresh parsley, finely chopped
- ¼ Cup olive oil
- ¼ Cup wine vinegar
- 1 Clove garlic, gently crushed
  Salt, and pepper mill
  Pinch of oregano
  Lettuce leaves

Combine beans, sausage, celery, pickles, tomato, onion, egg and parsley in a large salad bowl.

Blend the olive oil with vinegar, garlic clove and salt and freshly ground black pepper to taste and the oregano. When thoroughly blended discard the garlic clove and pour dressing over salad and toss thoroughly.

Chill the salad well before serving, and serve on crisp lettuce leaves on individual chilled salad plates.

LAMB SALAD

(Serves 4)

1 Cup cold cooked lamb, cut into 1-inch pieces
2 Cups romaine lettuce, torn into bite-size pieces
1 Green bell pepper, medium size, chopped coarsely
1 Tablespoon capers
3 Tablespoons olive oil
1 Tablespoon wine vinegar
½ Teaspoon fresh oregano, chopped fine
Salt, and pepper mill

In a chilled salad bowl combine the lamb, romaine, green bell pepper and capers.

Blend thoroughly the olive oil, vinegar, oregano, salt and freshly ground black pepper to taste.

Add dressing to salad and toss lightly.

Serve on individual cold salad plates.

LENTIL SALAD

(*Serves 4*)

2 Cups cooked lentils, drained and cooled
1 Tablespoon fresh parsley, finely chopped
1 Tablespoon capers
1 Tablespoon chives, finely chopped
1 Tablespoon dill pickle, finely chopped
3 Tablespoons olive oil
1 Tablespoon tarragon vinegar
3 Anchovy filets, cut into small pieces
Pepper mill
Crisp lettuce leaves

In a salad bowl combine the lentils with the parsley, capers, chives and pickle.

Blend thoroughly the olive oil, vinegar and anchovies.

Pour the dressing over the salad and toss well.

Season to taste with freshly ground black pepper.

Chill thoroughly.

Serve on lettuce leaves on cold salad plates.

STUFFED MAINE LOBSTER

(Serves 2)

2   Whole boiled Maine lobsters, chilled
⅔   Cup avocado, diced
1   Large fresh tomato, peeled and diced
½   Cup yogurt
⅛   Teaspoon Worcestershire sauce
1   Teaspoon fresh lemon juice
    Salt, and pepper mill
2   Teaspoons finely chopped chives

Split the lobsters in two, removing the claws and saving the shells. Remove sac and vein from each lobster. Remove meat from the lobsters and dice into ¼-inch cubes.

In a wooden salad bowl combine lobster meat with avocado, tomato, yogurt, Worcestershire sauce, lemon juice, salt and freshly ground black pepper to taste. Toss lightly.

Carefully spoon the lobster mixture into the lobster shells. Sprinkle with chives. Serve very cold.

LOBSTER SALAD DE LUXE

(*Serves 4*)

2 Lobster tails, boiled, cooled and cut into ½-inch pieces
½ Cup celery, thinly sliced
1 Head butter lettuce, torn into bite-size pieces
2 Hard-cooked egg yolks
1 Teaspoon dry mustard
3 Tablespoons olive oil
1 Tablespoon wine vinegar
1 Raw egg yolk
  Salt, and pepper mill

In a salad bowl combine the lobster meat with the celery, and lettuce.

Blend until smooth the yolks, mustard, oil, vinegar, raw egg yolk, salt and freshly ground black pepper to taste.

Add the dressing to the salad bowl and toss lightly.

Serve immediately on chilled salad plates.

LORENZO SALAD

(Serves 4-6)

1	Head romaine, medium size, torn into bite-size pieces
½	Cup celery, thinly sliced
1	Cup fresh pears, cut into ½-inch cubes
1	Cup fresh apples, cut into ½-inch cubes
1	Cup fresh oranges, cut into ½-inch cubes
½	Cup olive oil
¼	Cup vinegar
½	Cup chili sauce
½	Cup chopped watercress
	Salt, and pepper mill

In a salad bowl combine the romaine, celery, pears, apples and oranges.

In a smaller bowl blend until smooth the oil, vinegar, chili sauce, watercress and salt and freshly ground black pepper to taste.

Add dressing to the salad and toss lightly.

Serve on individual cold salad plates.

MUSHROOM SALAD

(*Serves 2*)

½ Pound fresh mushrooms, sliced
1 Tablespoon butter
½ Cup celery, thinly sliced
2 Tablespoons yogurt
½ Teaspoon tarragon vinegar
  Crisp lettuce leaves
4 Slices of fresh tomato
1 Teaspoon fresh parsley, chopped fine
  Salt, and pepper mill

Sauté mushrooms lightly in butter. Cool thoroughly.

Combine the mushrooms and celery in a salad bowl and toss gently.

Blend the yogurt with the vinegar until smooth.

Add dressing to salad and toss gently.

Serve on crisp lettuce leaves and garnish with tomato and parsley.

Season to taste with salt and freshly ground black pepper.

OYSTER SALAD

(Serves 4)

2 Cups fresh oysters
1 Cup celery, thinly sliced
1 Pickled cucumber, thinly sliced
  Salt, and pepper mill
2 Hard-cooked eggs, sliced
2 Tablespoons mayonnaise
1 Teaspoon fresh parsley, minced
1 Teaspoon gherkins, finely chopped
1 Teaspoon chives, finely chopped
1 Teaspoon capers, finely chopped
1 Teaspoon shallots, finely chopped
  Lettuce leaves

Scald the oysters in their own liquor until plump and frilled. Drain and chill thoroughly.

In a salad bowl combine the oysters with the celery, cucumber, salt and freshly ground black pepper to taste.

Add the eggs and toss lightly.

Blend the mayonnaise, parsley, gherkins, chives, capers and shallots until smooth.

Add to salad and toss gently.

Serve on crisp lettuce leaves on cold salad plates.

PARSNIP SALAD

(*Serves 4*)

- 1   Small head butter lettuce, torn into bite-size pieces
- 1   Cup raw parsnips, shredded
- ½   Cup celery, thinly sliced
- ⅓   Cup green bell pepper, chopped fine
- 1   Apple, unpeeled, cored and cut into small cubes
  Salt, and pepper mill
- 2   Tablespoons salad oil
- 1   Tablespoon wine vinegar
- 1   Tablespoon fresh cream

In a large wooden salad bowl combine the lettuce, parsnips, celery, green pepper, apple, salt and freshly ground black pepper to taste.

Blend the oil, vinegar and cream thoroughly.

Add to salad bowl and toss lightly.

Serve on individual cold salad plates.

PETER B. KYNE'S SALAD

(*Serves 4*)

- 2 Cloves garlic
- 1 Chapon* of French bread, toasted and rubbed well
     with garlic
- 1 Head romaine lettuce, torn into bite-size pieces
     Olive oil
     Salt, and pepper mill
     Dash paprika
- 2 Fresh lemons, juice only

Rub the inner surface of a wooden salad bowl with the garlic.

Place the chapon of French bread in the bowl, then add a few pieces of lettuce and a little olive oil and toss lightly. Keep adding lettuce and olive oil until the lettuce is used. After each addition, toss lightly but thoroughly. The amount of oil should be known by instinct. You can use too little olive oil, but not too much.

Season to taste with salt and freshly ground black pepper.

Add the paprika and lemon juice and toss thoroughly.

Set aside for 15 minutes before serving so that the flavor penetrates the romaine.

Serve on cold individual salad plates.

* The end or heel of French bread; see "Your Guide to the Perfect Salad."

POTATO SALAD,
AMERICAN STYLE

(Serves 4)

4 Medium potatoes
½ Cup mayonnaise
1 Bermuda onion, medium size, chopped fine
2 Stalks celery, chopped fine
1 Cucumber, diced
6 Small radishes, sliced
4 Hard-cooked eggs, chopped coarsely
1 Tablespoon parsley, chopped fine
Salt, and pepper mill

Boil potatoes until just tender. Skin and place in a larg
bowl. Break into chunks with two forks and add mayonnais
Add onion, cover and chill.
Add celery, cucumber, radishes, eggs and parsley. If nece
sary, add additional mayonnaise to bind.
Season to taste with salt and freshly ground black peppe
Toss thoroughly.
Chill thoroughly before serving.

POTATO SALAD SUPREME

(*Serves 6*)

6   Potatoes, boiled in jackets, peeled, cooled and
     thinly sliced
½   Bunch radishes, thinly sliced
1   Bermuda onion, medium size, grated
1   Cucumber, medium size, unpeeled, diced in ¼-inch
     cubes
1   Carrot, medium size, grated
2   Teaspoons parsley, chopped fine
½   Cup sour cream
¼   Cup vinegar
¼   Teaspoon paprika
     Salt, and pepper mill

Toss together lightly in a wooden salad bowl, potatoes,
radishes, onion, cucumber, carrot and parsley.

Blend until smooth sour cream, vinegar, paprika and salt
and freshly ground black pepper to taste.

Add dressing to salad and toss gently, but thoroughly.

Chill thoroughly before serving.

RUTHERFORD SALAD
WITH GOURMET DRESSING

(*Serves 4*)

1	Large head iceberg lettuce, torn into bite-size piec‹
4	Small tomatoes, quartered
12	Fresh pre-cooked asparagus spears, chilled
12	Whole pre-cooked prawns, peeled, de-veined and‍ chilled
1	Three-ounce package cream cheese
½	Teaspoon grated Bermuda onion
½	Teaspoon garlic salt
⅛	Teaspoon paprika
3	Ounces California white dinner wine
½	Cup sour cream
1	Tablespoon chili sauce
4½	Ounces undrained minced clams
¼	Cup finely chopped green onions
	Pepper mill

Mount lettuce in salad bowl with tomatoes, asparagus spea‍ and prawns.

In a smaller bowl, cream the cheese until soft. Blend grated onion, garlic salt, paprika and white wine.

Add the sour cream, chili sauce, clams and green onion‍ Emulsify well. Season to taste with freshly ground bla‹ pepper.

Add dressing to the salad and toss gently, trying not ‍ break the asparagus spears.

Mount salad on chilled salad plates and serve immediatel‍

SHRIMP SALAD

(Serves 4)

1   Cup fresh shrimp, cooked, cooled and coarsely
      chopped
½   Cup fresh mushrooms, sliced and sautéed lightly in
      butter
½   Cup fresh celery, thinly sliced
½   Cup fresh cauliflower flowerets, coarsely chopped
3   Tablespoons olive oil
1   Tablespoon wine vinegar
1   Tablespoon yogurt
½   Teaspoon curry powder
      Salt
      Lettuce leaves

Combine shrimp, mushrooms, celery and cauliflower in a
salad bowl and toss lightly.
Blend the oil, vinegar, yogurt, curry powder and salt to
taste, until smooth.
Add dressing to the salad and toss lightly.
Chill thoroughly before serving.
Serve on crisp lettuce leaves on chilled salad plates.

SPINACH AND BACON SALAD

(*Serves 6*)

4 Cups fresh spinach leaves, torn into bite-size pieces
3 Hard-cooked eggs, chopped coarsely
8 Slices bacon, diced, fried crisp and drained
½ Cup yogurt
1 Tablespoon grated Bermuda onion
½ Clove garlic, finely chopped
1 Teaspoon celery leaves, finely chopped
1 Teaspoon parsley, finely chopped
Salt, and pepper mill

In a wooden salad bowl combine the spinach, eggs and bacon.

In a smaller bowl, blend together until smooth, the yogurt, onion, garlic, celery leaves, parsley and salt and pepper to taste.

Add to salad bowl and toss lightly.

Serve on chilled salad plates.

SPINACH SALAD

(Serves 4)

2 Bunches fresh spinach leaves, torn into bite-size pieces
1 Large red apple, unpeeled, cored and diced into ½-inch cubes
2 Fresh green onions, thinly sliced
1 Fresh carrot, medium size, grated
2 Hard-cooked eggs, sliced ¼-inch thick
3 Tablespoons olive oil
1 Tablespoon wine vinegar
Salt, and pepper mill

In a large wooden salad bowl toss together lightly the spinach, apple, onions, carrot and eggs.

Blend the oil, vinegar, salt and freshly ground black pepper to taste.

Add the dressing to the salad and toss lightly.

Serve on chilled salad plates.

VICTOR'S
FLAMING SPINACH SALAD

(*Serves 4 to 6*)

2   Packages (10 ounces each) fresh young tender spinach

½   Pound bacon, diced

½   Cup red wine vinegar

3   Tablespoons Worcestershire sauce

1   Juicy lemon, cut in half; squeeze juice through napkin to hold back seeds and pulp

½   Cup sugar

¼   Cup Cognac or brandy

Remove stems from spinach leaves and discard. Wash leaves thoroughly and pat dry with clean cloth. Chill in refrigerator before using.

Sauté bacon in chafing dish over high flame until it just begins to brown. Add vinegar, Worcestershire sauce, lemon juice and sugar. Stir well until sugar is dissolved. When sauce begins to simmer, holding back diced bacon pieces, pour sauce over the young tender fresh spinach leaves. Do not be afraid of bruising the leaves, but bear down hard when tossing this salad in order that the main vein of leaves will break for dressing to penetrate as well as emulsify each young leaf. Divide spinach evenly on four salad plates and set aside in readiness.

While pan is getting hot and bacon pieces are browning, add Cognac or brandy with left hand; holding chafing dish with right hand and when alcoholic gas begins to sizzle upward, pull pan back toward you three to eight inches over flame and hold hand back aloof in order for gas cloud to ignite. While bacon is still flaming, ladle it evenly over the individual mounds of spinach on salad plates and serve immediately.

Under no circumstances is salt or pepper to be added during the creation of this salad, nor is it to be used while enjoying the full-bodied sweet and sour flavor. *So warn your guests!*

SPRING SALAD

(*Serves 8*)

1   Bunch fresh spinach, stems removed and leaves
    torn into bite-size pieces
1   Small head lettuce, torn into bite-size pieces
1   Bunch radishes, thinly sliced
1   Bunch fresh green onions, chopped fine
1   Cup celery, thinly sliced
1   Cup red cabbage, shredded fine
1   Cucumber, unpeeled, scored and thinly sliced
1   Green bell pepper, julienned
½   Bunch watercress, stems removed (use leaves only)
2   Avocados, peeled and sliced into eighths
2   Ounces bleu cheese, crumbled
1   Cup sour cream
    Juice of ½ fresh lemon
2   Tablespoons cider vinegar
1   Teaspoon sugar
1   Clove garlic, finely chopped
1   Teaspoon grated Bermuda onion
¼   Teaspoon monosodium glutamate
    Salt, and pepper mill
3   Fresh tomatoes, cut into small wedges

Combine all ingredients except tomatoes in a large wooden
salad bowl.

Blend until smooth the sour cream, lemon juice, vinegar,
sugar, garlic, onion, monosodium glutamate, salt and freshly
ground black pepper to taste.

Add dressing to the salad and toss carefully.

Serve on individual cold salad plates and garnish with
tomatoes.

STRING BEAN SALAD

(*Serves 4*)

- 2 Pounds fresh string beans, cut through center lengthwise and in 2-inch lengths
- 1 Large Italian onion, thinly sliced
  Salt, and pepper mill
  Pinch of paprika
- ½ Cup olive oil
- ½ Cup wine vinegar
- ½ Cup water
- 3 Cloves garlic, mashed
- 4 Fresh mint leaves, chopped fine
  Lettuce leaves

Cook string beans in salted water until tender. Drain and cool thoroughly.

Place beans in a large bowl and add onion, salt, freshly ground black pepper to taste, paprika, olive oil, vinegar, water, garlic and fresh mint leaves. Mix thoroughly.

Cover and thoroughly chill in the refrigerator.

Serve on crisp lettuce leaves.

SUMMER SALAD

(*Serves 4*)

1 Head lettuce, torn into bite-size pieces
½ Bunch mustard greens, torn into bite-size pieces
6 Radishes, thinly sliced
1 Cucumber, unpeeled, scored and thinly sliced
2 Hard-cooked eggs, sliced ¼-inch thick
3 Tablespoons olive oil
1 Tablespoon fresh lemon juice
1 Teaspoon sugar
Salt, and pepper mill

In a wooden salad bowl combine the lettuce with the mustard greens, radishes, cucumber and eggs.

Blend thoroughly the olive oil, lemon juice, sugar, salt and freshly ground black pepper to taste.

Add dressing to the salad and toss lightly.

Serve on cold salad plates.

SWEETBREADS SALAD

(*Serves 2*)

1 Pair large sweetbreads
1 Whole fresh lemon, cut in half
1 Cut celery, thinly sliced
  Salt, and pepper mill
2 Tablespoons yogurt
  Lettuce leaves

Parboil sweetbreads in water with lemon until tender. Drain and cool thoroughly. Remove the thin membrane and cut into 1-inch cubes.

In a wooden salad bowl combine the sweetbreads with the celery, salt and freshly ground black pepper to taste.

Add the yogurt and toss gently.

Serve on crisp lettuce leaves.

TOMATO-BASIL SALAD

(*Serves 6*)

4	Fresh tomatoes, sliced ¼-inch thick
1	Pimento, thinly sliced
2	Dill pickles, medium size, thinly sliced
¼	Cup celery, thinly sliced
¼	Cup chives, finely chopped
4	Sprigs fresh sweet basil, finely chopped
8	Thin slices ham, coarsely chopped
3	Tablespoons olive oil
1	Fresh lemon (juice only)
1	Tablespoon parsley, finely chopped
	Salt, and pepper mill
	Lettuce leaves

In a large wooden salad bowl combine the tomatoes, pimento, dill pickles, celery, chives and basil.

Blend the ham with oil, lemon juice, parsley, salt and freshly ground black pepper to taste.

Add dressing to the salad and toss lightly.

Serve on crisp lettuce leaves on individual chilled salad plates.

TOMATO-CHEESE SALAD

(*Serves 4*)

- 4 Fresh tomatoes, peeled and cut in wedges
- ½ Head butter lettuce, torn into bite-size pieces
  Parmesan cheese, grated
- 3 Tablespoons olive oil
- 1 Tablespoon fresh lemon juice
- 1 Tablespoon white wine
  Salt, and pepper mill
- ½ Teaspoon paprika
- ½ Teaspoon fresh sweet basil, chopped fine
  Crisp lettuce leaves

In a wooden salad bowl combine tomatoes and lettuce.
Add parmesan cheese to taste and toss lightly.

Blend thoroughly the olive oil, lemon juice, wine, salt
freshly ground black pepper to taste, paprika and basil.

Add dressing to the salad and toss lightly.

Serve on crisp lettuce leaves.

TOMATO SALAD

(*Serves 6*)

6   Fresh tomatoes, cut in wedges
1   Large Bermuda onion, thinly sliced
¼   Cup olive oil
    Salt, and pepper mill
2   Teaspoons fresh oregano, finely chopped

In a wooden salad bowl, combine the tomatoes, onion, olive
il, salt and freshly ground black pepper to taste. Toss gently.
Sprinkle with oregano.
Chill thoroughly before serving.

TUNA-BEAN SALAD

(*Serves 4*)

1   Cup tuna fish, flaked
1   Cup cooked lima beans, chilled
2   Hard-cooked eggs, coarsely chopped
⅓   Cup nuts, chopped coarsely
½   Dill pickle, chopped fine
1   Tablespoon chives, chopped fine
½   Cup mayonnaise
    Salt, and pepper mill
    Lettuce leaves

Combine tuna, beans, eggs, nuts, pickle and chives in a
alad bowl.
Add mayonnaise and toss lightly.
Season to taste with salt and freshly ground black pepper.
Serve on lettuce leaves on chilled salad plates.

TUNA SALAD

(*Serves 4*)

- 1   Cup tuna fish, flaked in large pieces
- 2   Hard-cooked eggs, chopped coarsely
- ½   Cup walnuts, coarsely chopped
- 1   Cup cooked Chinese peas, cooled and drained
- ½   Dill pickle, chopped fine
- 2   Teaspoons chives, chopped fine
- 1   Tablespoon capers
      Salt, and pepper mill
- ¼   Cup sour cream
      Crisp lettuce leaves

In a salad bowl combine the tuna fish with the eggs, walnuts, peas, pickle, chives and capers.

Season to taste with salt and freshly ground black pepper. Add sour cream and toss lightly.

Serve on lettuce leaves.

SENATE SALAD

(Serves 4)

2 Cups cold cooked lobster meat, chopped coarsely
1 Cup iceberg lettuce, torn into bite-size pieces
1 Cup romaine lettuce, torn into bite-size pieces
½ Cup watercress leaves
1 Cup celery, sliced thin
¼ Cup whole fresh green onions, chopped fine
2 Fresh tomatoes, medium size, peeled and diced
5 Large ripe olives, pitted and sliced
1 Avocado, quartered and sliced
½ Grapefruit, sectioned and coarsely chopped
   Salt, and pepper mill

Toss together in a wooden salad bowl the lobster, iceberg and romaine lettuce, watercress, celery, onions, tomatoes, olives, avocado and grapefruit. Season to taste with salt and freshly ground black pepper.

Toss with your favorite dressing and serve immediately.

WATERCRESS AND BACON SALAD

(Serves 4)

- 1 Large bunch watercress, torn into bite-size pieces
- 6 Slices bacon, diced, fried until crisp and drained
- 4 Hard-cooked eggs, coarsely chopped
  Salt, and pepper mill
- 2 Tablespoons Roquefort cheese, crumbled
- ½ Fresh lemon (juice only)
- ¼ Teaspoon dry mustard
- 1 Tablespoon olive oil
- ¼ Cup sour cream

In a wooden salad bowl combine the watercress, bacon and eggs.

Season to taste with salt and freshly ground black pepper.

Blend the cheese, lemon juice, mustard, oil and sour cream until smooth.

Add dressing to the salad and toss lightly.

Serve on cold salad plates.

WILTED ENDIVE SALAD

(Serves 4)

- 1 Large head curly endive, torn into bite-size pieces
- 2 Tablespoons chives, chopped fine
  Salt, and pepper mill
- 4 Slices bacon, diced
- 3 Tablespoons cider vinegar
- 3 Hard-cooked eggs, sliced

Mix the endive with the chives in a wooden salad bowl.

Season to taste with salt and freshly ground black pepper.

Fry bacon until crisp. Add vinegar, bring to a boil and pour over the salad. Toss quickly.

Add eggs and mix lightly.

Serve at once.

WILTED LETTUCE SALAD

(Serves 4)

3 Slices bacon, diced
1 Whole fresh raw egg, slightly beaten
½ Cup vinegar
1 Bermuda onion, medium size, chopped fine
½ Teaspoon sugar
  Salt, and pepper mill
  Pinch of paprika
1 Head leaf lettuce, torn into bite-size pieces
2 Hard-cooked eggs, diced

Fry bacon until crisp and remove to paper towels to drain.
Mix together in a bowl the slightly beaten egg, vinegar,
onion, sugar, salt and freshly ground black pepper to taste,
and paprika. Add to bacon fat and cook over low heat, stirring constantly until thickened and smooth.

In a salad bowl combine the lettuce with the bacon and
diced eggs. Add the dressing and toss together lightly until
well mixed.

Serve immediately.

WILTED LETTUCE SALAD

Simple Style
(Serves 4)

1   Large head leaf lettuce, torn into bite-size pieces
1   Cup fresh green onions, chopped fine
     Salt, and pepper mill
½   Cup bacon, diced
¼   Cup vinegar

In a salad bowl combine the lettuce and onions.

Season to taste with salt and freshly ground black pepper.

Set the salad bowl over hot water (a teakettle is fine) while preparing the dressing.

Fry the bacon until crisp and remove to a paper towel to drain.

To the fat remaining in the pan, add the vinegar and bring to a boil, then pour, sizzling hot, over the lettuce and onions in the bowl and toss thoroughly.

Sprinkle the crisp bacon bits on top and serve immediately.

WINTER SALAD

(*Serves 4*)

3	Large sweet Spanish onions, peeled and thinly sliced in rings
1	Cup sour cream
2	Tablespoons honey-flavored French mustard
1	Teaspoon salt
1¼	Teaspoons freshly ground black pepper
1	Teaspoon paprika

Separate onion slices into rings and place in salad bowl.

Combine the sour cream, mustard, salt, pepper and paprika and blend until smooth.

Add dressing to the onions in the salad bowl and toss lightly.

Serve immediately on chilled salad plates.

CANADA

~

FISH SALAD

(*Serves 6*)

1	Pound cod, haddock or other salt-water, white-meat fish
1½	Cups water
1	Bermuda onion, medium size, thinly sliced
1	Teaspoon salt
2	Apples, peeled and diced
½	Cup cucumbers, peeled and diced
½	Cup celery, diced
2	Teaspoons parsley, chopped fine
½	Teaspoon Worcestershire sauce
½	Teaspoon Bermuda onion, grated
3	Tablespoons yogurt
2	Hard-cooked eggs, chopped fine
	Crisp lettuce leaves
	Salt, and pepper mill

Wash the fish and place in a saucepan with the water, sliced onion and salt. Bring to a boil and cook over medium heat for 20 minutes. Drain well, flake and cool in the refrigerator for 2 hours.

Place the flaked fish in a large salad bowl. Add the apples, cucumbers and celery and mix well. Then add the parsley, Worcestershire sauce, grated onion and yogurt. Toss lightly and serve on crisp lettuce leaves. Sprinkle with the chopped eggs. Let each guest season his own salad with salt and freshly ground black pepper.

CANADA

CHINOOK SALAD

(*Serves 4*)

½   Head lettuce, torn into bite-size pieces
½   Cup cooked cold beets, julienned
½   Cup celery, thinly sliced
 1   Cup fresh salmon, cooked, cooled and flaked
 3   Tablespoons olive oil
 1   Tablespoon tarragon vinegar
    Salt, and pepper mill
 2   Hard-cooked eggs, chopped fine

In a wooden salad bowl, combine the lettuce, beets, celery and salmon.

Blend the olive oil, vinegar, salt and freshly ground black pepper to taste and eggs, until smooth.

Add dressing to the salad and toss lightly.

Chill thoroughly before serving.

SALAD DRESSINGS

To make a good salad is to be a brilliant diplomatist; the problem is entirely the same in both cases — to know exactly how much oil one must put with one's vinegar.
OSCAR WILDE

SALAD DRESSINGS

The mixing of greens of the field in a large container, the first "Salad Bowl," was an old Arabian custom. They used olive oil for the dressing which was warmed by the rays of the sun. Now, of course, we chill our dressing. Later, the Greeks created new recipes, developed new herbs and introduced new spices. The Romans took up this delicacy and greatly improved the dressing. It was a princess of the famous Florentine Medici family, which had so much power in Tuscany in the fifteenth century, who introduced salads to the French.

Finally the idea of salads came to America. Here certain groups used salads for a great number of years. Bohemians who migrated to this country were talented salad makers and the old German families have used salads for centuries, their seasoning for salads being most outstanding.

Salad dressings should complement a salad, be tart when the salad is bland, unctuous when it's light, and bland when it's forthright. Too little dressing looks skimpy, but an excess is wasteful and drowns ingredients. Allow one tablespoon of dressing for each serving.

SIDNEY SMITH'S RECIPE
FOR SALAD DRESSING

Two boiled potatoes, strained through a kitchen sieve,
Softness and smoothness to the salad give;
Of mordant mustard take a single spoon—
Distrust the condiment that bites too soon;
Yet deem it not, though man of taste, a fault,
To add a double quantity of salt.
Four times the spoon, with oil of Lucca crown,
And twice with vinegar procured from town;
True taste requires it, and your poet begs
The pounded yellow of two well-boiled eggs.
Let onion atoms lurk within the bowl,
And, scarce suspected, animate the whole;
And lastly, in the flavored compound toss
A magic teaspoonful of anchovy sauce.
Oh, great and glorious! oh, herbaceous meat!
'Twould tempt the dying anchorite to eat;
Back to the world he'd turn his weary soul,
And plunge his fingers in the salad bowl.

ANCHOVY DRESSING

(Makes 1½ Cups)

1   Small can anchovies, drained and chopped fine
¼   Cup olive oil
¾   Cup salad oil
¼   Cup fresh lemon juice
1   Teaspoon dry mustard
1   Teaspoon paprika
½   Small white onion, finely chopped

Put all ingredients in glass container of an electric blender, cover and blend for about two minutes until smooth, or the ingredients may be blended together in a small bowl.

BACON DRESSING

(Makes ½ Cup)

3   Strips bacon cut into small pieces
½   Teaspoon sugar
    Salt, and pepper mill
2   Tablespoons sharp vinegar

Fry bacon in a skillet over a low flame until crisp.

Add sugar, salt and freshly ground black pepper to taste, and vinegar to the hot bacon fat in the skillet, then bring to a boil.

When sizzling hot, pour over salad greens immediately, toss and serve.

Excellent over torn greens or vegetables such as green beans, bean sprouts or even potatoes.

BOILED DRESSING

(Makes 1½ Cups)

¼ Cup butter
1 Tablespoon flour
½ Cup cider vinegar
½ Cup dry white wine
½ Cup granulated sugar
2 Teaspoons prepared mustard
  Salt, and pepper mill

Melt butter in saucepan. Blend in flour and stir until smooth.

Combine vinegar, wine, sugar, mustard, salt and freshly ground black pepper to taste.

Stir into butter-flour mixture. Simmer until thickened, stirring constantly. Cool, but do not chill.

This dressing is ideal for fruit salads. It may be used for other salads by omitting the sugar.

CELERY SEED DRESSING

(Makes ½ Cup)

½ Teaspoon dry mustard
  Salt, and pepper mill
1 Teaspoon Bermuda onion, chopped fine
2 Tablespoons vinegar
6 Tablespoons salad oil
1 Teaspoon celery seeds

Blend the mustard, salt and freshly ground black pepper to taste, onion and half of the vinegar, until smooth.

Gradually add the oil, stirring constantly.

Add the remaining vinegar and the celery seeds and blend until smooth.

CHIFFONADE DRESSING

(Makes 1½ Cups)

¼ Cup olive oil
¾ Cup salad oil
¼ Cup vinegar
1 Teaspoon salt
1 Teaspoon sugar
1 Teaspoon dry mustard
1 Teaspoon paprika
1 Teaspoon onion juice
1 Tablespoon green bell pepper, diced fine
1 Hard-cooked egg, chopped fine

Mix all ingredients thoroughly in a bowl or electric blender until smooth.

CURRY DRESSING

(Makes 1 Cup)

½ Teaspoon garlic salt
1 Teaspoon freshly ground black pepper
1 Teaspoon sugar
1 Teaspoon dry mustard
1 Teaspoon curry powder
¼ Cup red wine vinegar
½ Teaspoon soy sauce
⅔ Cup salad oil

Combine all the ingredients in a glass jar with a tight-fitting cover.
Shake well until blended thoroughly.
Chill several hours before using.

ESCAROLE DRESSING

(Makes ¾ Cup)

6   Tablespoons bleu cheese, crumbled
3   Tablespoons wine vinegar
      Dash of steak sauce (Escoffier Sauce Diable)
8   Tablespoons olive oil
1   Clove of garlic, crushed gently
      Salt, and pepper mill

Blend the cheese, vinegar, steak sauce, olive oil and garlic until smooth.

Remove garlic before adding the dressing to the salad.

Season to taste with salt and freshly ground black pepper.

Preparing a quantity of French dressing ahead saves time, but to avoid wilting it should not be put on the salad until just before serving. Lacking any made-ahead French dressing, just add oil and vinegar and seasonings in any desired proportion directly to the salad. Toss, correct seasoning to taste and serve.

Olive oil has no peer for French dressing. Be sure the olive oil you choose is not too strong for your palate. In the interest of economy, it may be mixed with a flavorless oil such as corn or cottonseed. Wine vinegar, red or white, makes the best French dressing. Depending upon flavor desired, lemon juice and sharp vinegar also may be used.

PIQUANT FRENCH DRESSING

(Makes ¾ Cup)

1	Tablespoon salt
½	Teaspoon sugar
⅛	Teaspoon freshly ground black pepper
¼	Teaspoon paprika
1	Teaspoon prepared mustard
½	Teaspoon onion juice
½	Clove garlic, peeled and mashed gently
1	Tablespoon boiling water
½	Cup olive or salad oil as preferred
3½	Tablespoons wine or tarragon vinegar

Combine the seasonings and add the boiling water to dissolve them.

Add the oil and vinegar. Blend thoroughly.

Beat well before serving.

BASIC FRENCH DRESSING

(Makes 1 Cup)

- ¾   Cup salad oil or olive oil
- ¼   Cup vinegar
- 1   Teaspoon salt
- 1   Teaspoon sugar
- ½   Teaspoon paprika
- ¼   Teaspoon dry mustard
  - Dash of freshly ground black pepper

Combine all the ingredients in a glass jar with a tight-fitting cover.

Shake until thoroughly blended. Chill.

Shake well each time before using.

CLASSIC FRENCH DRESSING

(Makes 1¼ Cups)

- 1   Cup olive oil or salad oil
- 3   Tablespoons tarragon vinegar
- 3   Tablespoons garlic vinegar
- 1   Teaspoon salt
- 1   Teaspoon freshly ground black pepper

Combine all the ingredients thoroughly in a glass jar with a tight-fitting cover.

Keep under refrigeration in the jar.

Shake thoroughly each time before using.

CRYSTAL FRENCH DRESSING

(Makes 1¼ Cups)

¼ Cup sugar
1 Teaspoon celery seed
½ Teaspoon salt
1 Teaspoon dry mustard
¼ Cup vinegar
1 Cup salad oil

Combine the sugar, celery seed, salt and mustard.
Add the vinegar and mix until well blended.
Slowly add the oil, beating constantly.
The dressing is very thick when all the oil is added.
Chill before serving.

FRENCH DRESSING
AUX FINES HERBES

(Makes 2 Cups)

¼   Cup garlic vinegar
¼   Cup sweet basil vinegar
¼   Cup eschalot vinegar
¼   Cup tarragon vinegar
½   Cup peanut oil
½   Cup olive oil
2   Teaspoons Beau Monde seasoning salt
2   Teaspoons Mei Yen seasoning powder
1½ Teaspoons paprika
1   Teaspoon freshly ground black pepper
¾   Teaspoon onion powder
½   Teaspoon garlic powder
¼   Teaspoon oregano, pulverized
1   Bay leaf

In a glass jar with a tight-fitting cover mix the vinegars and oils.

Add the dry ingredients and shake thoroughly.

Store in refrigerator for future use and shake well before using each time.

ROQUEFORT FRENCH DRESSING

(Makes 1½ Cups)

1¼ Cups salad oil
  3 Tablespoons cider vinegar
1½ Teaspoons salt
  ¼ Teaspoon freshly ground black pepper
  ¼ Teaspoon paprika
  ½ Teaspoon celery salt
  1 Tablespoon fresh lemon juice
  1 Teaspoon A-1 sauce
     Dash Tabasco sauce
  ½ Cup crumbled Roquefort cheese

Combine all ingredients except the cheese. Beat until smooth and well blended.

Gradually add the dressing to the cheese, blending until smooth after each addition.

Chill. Shake well before serving.

WINE FRENCH DRESSING

(Makes 1½ Cups)

  1 Cup dry red table wine
  1 Cup olive oil
1½ Teaspoons salt
  ½ Teaspoon coarse ground black pepper
  ¼ Teaspoon dry mustard
  ½ Teaspoon Worcestershire sauce
     Garlic, to taste

Combine ingredients in a pint jar and shake vigorously. Chill several hours so flavors can blend. Shake well before using.

FRENCH CHEESE DRESSING

(*Makes 2 Cups*)

¼ Pound bleu cheese, crumbled
¼ Cup grated parmesan cheese
¼ Cup red wine vinegar
¼ Cup Burgundy wine
1 Teaspoon salt
½ Teaspoon freshly ground black pepper
1 Teaspoon paprika
½ Teaspoon Worcestershire sauce
1 Clove garlic, chopped fine
1 Cup salad oil

Blend the bleu cheese with the parmesan cheese.

Gradually blend in the red wine vinegar and wine.

Add salt, pepper, paprika, Worcestershire sauce, garlic and salad oil.

Shake or beat thoroughly.

SPICY FRENCH DRESSING

(*Makes 1¾ Cups*)

1 Teaspoon salt
1 Teaspoon sugar
1 Tablespoon freshly ground black pepper
2 Teaspoons paprika
1 Cup olive or salad oil
¼ Cup tarragon vinegar
¼ Cup garlic vinegar
¼ Cup eschalot vinegar

Blend dry ingredients in a jar with a tight-fitting cover.

Add oil and the vinegars. Shake thoroughly.

Shake well each time before using.

Serve with green salads.

VARIATIONS OF FRENCH DRESSING

GARLIC FRENCH DRESSING: Add a clove of peeled mashed garlic to the French dressing.

MUSTARD FRENCH DRESSING: Add ¼ teaspoon dry mustard to the seasonings for French dressing.

INDIA FRENCH DRESSING: Add 2 tablespoons chutney, 2 hard-cooked eggs, finely chopped, and ½ teaspoon curry powder to the French dressing.

MALAYAN DRESSING: Add a little curry powder and some finely chopped garlic to the French dressing.

FRUIT SALAD DRESSING—I

(Makes ⅓ Cup)

- 6 Tablespoons peanut oil
- 2 Tablespoons fresh lemon or fresh lime juice
- ⅓ Teaspoon salt
  Dash of freshly ground black pepper
- 1 Tablespoon honey

Blend all the ingredients together thoroughly.
Chill and mix thoroughly before using.

FRUIT SALAD DRESSING—II

(Makes 1 Cup)

- 2 Tablespoons fresh lemon juice
- ½ Cup heavy cream
- ¼ Teaspoon salt
- ⅛ Teaspoon ginger
- 3 Tablespoons confectioners' sugar
- 1 Avocado, peeled and diced

Mix all ingredients in a bowl or electric blender until
smooth and fluffy.

Chill thoroughly before serving with fresh fruit.

For a more delicate dressing, fold in an additional ¼
cup cream, whipped with a mixer or rotary beater.

MINT FRUIT SALAD DRESSING

(Makes ¾ Cup)

- 1   Teaspoon fresh mint, chopped fine
- ½   Teaspoon fresh oregano, chopped fine
- 4   Tablespoons olive oil
- 3   Tablespoons fresh lemon juice
- 1   Clove garlic, chopped fine
- 1   Fresh whole raw egg, beaten lightly
      Salt, and pepper mill

Thoroughly blend the mint with oregano, olive oil, lemon juice, garlic and egg.

Season to taste with salt and freshly ground black pepper.

GORGONZOLA CHEESE DRESSING

(Makes ¾ Cup)

- ½   Teaspoon dry mustard
- ¼   Teaspoon salt
- 1   Clove garlic, cut in half
- 4   Tablespoons wine vinegar
- ½   Cup olive oil
- 2   Ounces Gorgonzola cheese, crumbled

Mix mustard, salt and garlic thoroughly.

Add vinegar and blend thoroughly. Add oil, stirring until well blended.

Add the cheese and blend thoroughly.

Keep in a jar in a cool place. Shake well before using each time.

IMPERIAL DRESSING

(Makes 2¾ Cups)

¼	Cup brown sugar
1½	Teaspoons salt
⅛	Teaspoon freshly ground black pepper
1	Teaspoon onion salt
½	Teaspoon celery seed
3	Drops Tabasco sauce
1	Teaspoon paprika
½	Teaspoon fresh dill, finely chopped
½	Cup red wine vinegar
1	Cup catsup
1	Cup olive oil
3	Tablespoons capers
1	Teaspoon juice from capers
2	Teaspoons Worcestershire sauce
1 or 2	Cloves garlic (on toothpick)

In a saucepan simmer together the brown sugar, salt, pepper, onion salt, celery seed, Tabasco sauce, paprika, dill and vinegar until thoroughly heated and blended.

Cool for 10 minutes.

Blend in the catsup, olive oil, capers and juice and Worcestershire sauce. Add garlic.

Cool dressing at room temperature for 1 hour.

Refrigerate until ready to use. Shake well before using each time.

INDIA DRESSING

(*Makes 1 Cup*)

- 2   Hard-cooked eggs (yolks only)
      Pinch of salt
- 1   Teaspoon powdered sugar
      Dash paprika, cayenne and white pepper
- 1   Tablespoon strained lemon juice
- 2   Tablespoons tarragon vinegar
- ¼   Cup olive oil
- 1   Tablespoon red pimento, finely chopped
- 1   Tablespoon green bell pepper, finely chopped
- 1   Tablespoon pickled beets, finely chopped
- 1   Teaspoon fresh parsley, finely chopped
- 1   Tablespoon walnut meats, finely chopped

Press egg yolks through a fine sieve.

Combine the egg yolks with the salt, sugar, paprika, cayenne pepper, white pepper, lemon juice, vinegar and olive oil. Blend thoroughly.

Add pimento, green pepper, beets, parsley and walnut meats. Stir well and chill.

ITALIAN FRENCH DRESSING

(*Makes 2¼ Cups*)

- 6 Tablespoons Roquefort cheese, crumbled
- 2 Tablespoons grated Bermuda onion
- ¼ Cup fresh parsley, finely chopped
- ¼ Cup red wine vinegar
- ¼ Cup fresh lemon juice
- 4 Anchovy filets, finely cut
- ½ Teaspoon freshly ground black pepper
- ¾ Teaspoon salt
- Dash garlic powder
- 1 Teaspoon Worcestershire sauce
- 1½ Cups olive or salad oil

Combine all ingredients, adding the oil last. Beat until thoroughly blended.

Store in refrigerator in glass jars with tight-fitting covers for future use. Beat or shake well each time before using.

LEMON CREAM SALAD DRESSING

(*Makes 1¼ Cups*)

- ½ Tablespoon fresh lemon juice
- 2 Raw egg yolks
- ½ Tablespoon honey
- 1 Cup soured cream

Beat the lemon juice into the egg yolks. Stir in the honey and add the soured cream. Blend until smooth.

Recommended for fruit salads.

MAYONNAISE

Mayonnaise is basically composed of egg, oil and acid. Spices add piquancy. Whole eggs may be used, but mayonnaise will be richer and more flavorful with the yolk alone. Strictly fresh eggs do not make as stable a product as their elders. Recipes with a French background always specify oil—olive, but it is far more costly than corn and cottonseed oil. In addition, if a delicately flavored olive oil is used, the sharp spices will mask it, while a lustier olive oil may be overpowering in flavor. Sharp vinegar is preferable for this piquant dressing because wine vinegar is too bland and lemon juice doesn't keep.

Mayonnaise is known technically as a stable emulsion. To help keep it together, beat ingredients in a narrow bowl with a rounded bottom and sloping sides. A rotary beater, and electric mixer or a blender may be used. Beat oil in completely after each addition. Intermittent beating is as effective as continuous beating.

To Repair Broken Mayonnaise.   If separation should occur either during preparation or storage, beat an egg yolk and add the oil gradually as directed above until the mixture begins to thicken. Then add the separated mayonnaise gradually as if it were oil. When all the broken mayonnaise has been beaten in, add more oil, if necessary, to achieve desired consistency. Correct seasoning.

MAYONNAISE

(*Makes 2 Cups*)

1½	Cups salad oil
1	Teaspoon powdered sugar
¾	Teaspoon salt
⅛	Teaspoon cayenne pepper
¼	Teaspoon dry mustard
2	Fresh egg yolks
1½	Tablespoons fresh lemon juice
1½	Tablespoons vinegar

Measure the oil into a pitcher, then separately mix the dry ingredients. Add the egg yolks and beat until slightly thickened.

Add the lemon juice and vinegar gradually.

Using a hand egg beater, beat in the oil, one teaspoon at a time. When thick the oil may be added more rapidly, taking care to beat the mixture thoroughly after each addition.

When finished, 1 tablespoon of boiling water should be beaten in.

If stored in a tightly covered glass jar in a cool place, it will keep indefinitely.

MAYONNAISE RAVIGOTE

(*Makes 1½ Cups*)

1   Cup freshly made mayonnaise
2   Anchovy filets, finely chopped
1   Hard-cooked egg, chopped fine
2   Tablespoons capers
2   Tablespoons fresh chervil, finely chopped
2   Tablespoons fresh parsley, finely chopped
2   Tablespoons shallots, finely chopped
2   Tablespoons Bermuda onion, finely chopped
¼   Cup dry white wine
1   Tablespoon fresh lemon juice

Blend the mayonnaise, anchovies and egg thoroughly.

Cook together the capers, chervil, parsley, shallots and onion in the wine and lemon juice for 15 minutes. Cool and combine with the mayonnaise.

Chill well before serving.

MAYONNAISE TARRAGON

1   Cup mayonnaise
1   Tablespoon tomato ketchup
1   Teaspoon fresh tarragon, finely chopped
1   Teaspoon fresh lemon juice

Blend all ingredients together until smooth.

MAYONNAISE HORSERADISH

1   Cup mayonnaise
1   Cup caviar
1   Tablespoon fresh horseradish

Blend all ingredients together thoroughly.

MAYONNAISE CREAM

1   Cup mayonnaise
¼   Cup thick soured cream

Blend ingredients together thoroughly until smooth.

THOUSAND ISLAND DRESSING

1   Cup mayonnaise
5   Tablespoons chili sauce
½   Tablespoon chives, finely chopped
1   Whole pimento, finely chopped

Combine and blend ingredients thoroughly.

PIMENTO CHEESE DRESSING

(Makes 1 Cup)

1   Package pimento cheese (3¼ ounces)
⅓   Cup salad oil
2   Tablespoons lemon juice
¼   Cup sherry wine
2   Tablespoons fresh parsley, finely chopped
½   Teaspoon Worcestershire sauce
¼   Teaspoon onion salt
¼   Teaspoon garlic salt
¼   Teaspoon freshly ground black pepper

In a bowl mash the cheese with a fork and gradually blend in the oil, lemon juice and wine and stir until smooth.

Add the parsley, Worcestershire sauce, onion salt, garlic salt and pepper and mix until smooth.

Recommended for hearts-of-lettuce or with any fruit or vegetable that takes kindly to a cheese flavor.

RELISH CHEESE DRESSING

(Makes ⅓ Cup)

3   Tablespoons cream or cottage cheese
2   Tablespoons minced pickle relish
⅓   Cup salad oil
2½   Tablespoons sweet pickle vinegar

Place the cheese and relish in a bowl and gradually work in the oil and vinegar. Stir until the dressing is thick and creamy.

Recommended for use with vegetable or sliced tomato salad.

REMOULADE DRESSING

(Makes 1½ Cups)

- 1   Cup freshly made mayonnaise
- ¼   Cup sour pickles, finely chopped
- 1   Tablespoon capers, finely chopped
- 1   Teaspoon prepared mustard
- ½   Teaspoon fresh parsley, finely chopped
- ½   Teaspoon fresh tarragon, finely chopped
- ½   Teaspoon fresh chervil, finely chopped

Combine all the ingredients in a bowl and blend until smooth.

ROQUEFORT DRESSING

(Makes 1½ Cups)

- 1   Clove garlic
- ½   Teaspoon salt
- 2   Tablespoons Roquefort cheese
- 2   Teaspoons Worcestershire sauce
- 1   Fresh lemon, juice only
- ½   Teaspoon paprika
- ½   Teaspoon dry mustard
- 3   Drops Tabasco sauce
- 1   Tablespoon olive oil
- 1   Teaspoon wine vinegar
- 1   Cup sour cream

Mash garlic in bowl with salt. Add cheese and mash thoroughly.

Add Worcestershire sauce, lemon juice, paprika, mustard, Tabasco sauce, olive oil and wine vinegar and blend thoroughly until it has a pasty-fine texture.

Add sour cream and blend until smooth.

RUSSIAN DRESSING

(Makes 1¼ Cups)

1 Cup freshly made mayonnaise
3 Tablespoons chili sauce
1 Teaspoon pimentos, finely chopped
1 Teaspoon chives, finely chopped
3 Tablespoons caviar

Combine all the ingredients in a bowl and blend until smooth.

SOUR CREAM DRESSING

(Makes 1 Cup)

1 Cup sour cream
1 Tablespoon cider vinegar
1 Tablespoon fresh lemon juice
1 Tablespoon Bermuda onion, finely chopped
Salt, and pepper mill
Sugar

Blend until smooth the sour cream, vinegar, lemon juice, onion, salt, freshly ground black pepper and sugar to taste.
Excellent with cabbage or sliced cucumbers.

SOUTHERN SALAD DRESSING

(Makes 1½ Cups)

¾ Cup salad oil
¼ Cup sugar
¼ Cup vinegar
2 Ounces Southern Comfort
1 Teaspoon salt
1 Teaspoon dry mustard
1 Teaspoon paprika

Mix thoroughly with electric beater until smooth.

Store in refrigerator for future use. Shake well before using each time.

VINAIGRETTE DRESSING

(Makes ⅓ Cup)

1 Teaspoon salt
¼ Teaspoon freshly ground black pepper
1 Tablespoon wine vinegar
3 Tablespoons vegetable oil, or olive oil
1 Teaspoon shallots, finely chopped
1 Teaspoon fresh parsley, finely chopped

Combine the salt, pepper and vinegar in a bowl and stir until the salt is dissolved.

Blend in the oil thoroughly.

Add the shallots and parsley and mix well.

Excellent for all green salads, also good on cold meats.

WESTERN DRESSING

(Makes ¾ Cup)

- 2 Tablespoons honey
- 1 Teaspoon horseradish
- 1 Teaspoon dry mustard blended smooth with wine vinegar
- 1 Teaspoon paprika
- 6 Tablespoons herb vinegar
- 3 Tablespoons fresh lemon juice
- 1 Tablespoon grated Bermuda onion
- 4 Tablespoons vegetable oil
  Salt, and pepper mill

Blend until smooth honey, horseradish, mustard and paprika.

Gradually add the vinegar, lemon juice, onion and oil.

Season to taste with salt and freshly ground black pepper.

YOGURT DRESSING

Greek Style
(Makes 1 Cup)

- 1 Cup yogurt
- 1 Garlic clove, chopped fine
- ¼ Teaspoon oregano
- 1 Tablespoon olive oil
  Salt, and pepper mill
  Juice of 1 fresh lime or lemon

Blend until smooth yogurt, garlic, oregano, olive oil, salt and freshly ground black pepper to taste.

Add the juice of lime or lemon and blend until smooth.

YOGURT DRESSING

(Makes 1⅓ Cups)

- ¼ Cup Bermuda onion, finely chopped
- ½ Clove garlic, finely chopped
- ¼ Cup celery leaves, finely chopped
- ¼ Cup fresh parsley, finely chopped
- 1 Teaspoon salt
- 2 Teaspoons sugar
- 1 Tablespoon tomato paste
- 1 Cup yogurt

Combine all ingredients in a bowl and blend thoroughly until smooth.

YOGURT SUPREME DRESSING

(Makes 1¼ Cups)

- 1 Cup yogurt
- 1 Teaspoon fresh lemon juice
- ½ Teaspoon chives, finely chopped
- ½ Teaspoon paprika
- ½ Teaspoon dry mustard
- ½ Teaspoon salt

Combine all the ingredients in a bowl and mix well until thoroughly blended.

Chill thoroughly before using.

WINE DRESSINGS

ROQUEFORT WINE DRESSING

(Makes ¾ Cup)

¼ Cup Roquefort cheese, crumbled
¼ Cup olive oil
2 Tablespoons wine vinegar
2 Tablespoons Burgundy wine
½ Teaspoon Worcestershire sauce
Salt, and pepper mill

Mash the cheese with a fork in a medium size bowl.
Blend in the oil, vinegar and wine.
Add Worcestershire sauce, salt and freshly ground black
epper to taste. Blend until smooth.
Excellent on tomatoes.

SHERRY FRESH FRUIT
SALAD DRESSING

(Makes ½ Cup)

2 Tablespoons butter
1 Teaspoon flour
3 Tablespoons cider vinegar
3 Tablespoons sherry wine
1 Tablespoon granulated sugar
½ Teaspoon prepared mustard
Salt, and pepper mill

Melt butter in small saucepan.
Stir in flour and blend until smooth.
Combine vinegar, wine, sugar, mustard, salt and freshly
ound black pepper to taste.
Stir into butter-flour mixture. Simmer until thickened, stir-
ng constantly. Cool, but do not chill.
Serve over fresh fruits.

SHERRY LOUIS DRESSING

(Makes 1¾ Cups)

1   Cup freshly made mayonnaise
½   Cup chili sauce
3   Tablespoons sherry wine
1   Hard-cooked egg, chopped fine
¼   Cup ripe olives, chopped fine
½   Teaspoon Worcestershire sauce
    Salt, and pepper mill

Blend thoroughly the mayonnaise, chili sauce, wine, egg, olives, Worcestershire sauce, salt and freshly ground black pepper to taste.

Chill thoroughly before using.

Serve with crab, shrimp or lobster salads.

SOUR CREAM (WINE FLAVOR) DRESSING

(Makes 1¼ Cups)

1   Cup sour cream
3   Tablespoons sauterne wine
2   Tablespoons sweet basil vinegar
1   Teaspoon salt
½   Teaspoon freshly ground black pepper
1   Tablespoon sugar
⅛   Teaspoon cayenne pepper

Combine all ingredients and blend until smooth.
Excellent for cabbage slaw salad.

HOW TO MAKE YOUR OWN

Yogurt
Skim Milk Yogurt
Italian Red Wine Vinegar
Italian White Wine Vinegar
Chili Vinegar
Herb Vinegar
Fines Herbes Vinegar—I
Fines Herbes Vinegar—II
Nasturtium Vinegar
Tarragon Vinegar—I
Tarragon Vinegar—II
Garlic Mayonnaise Toast
Garlic Cheese Toast

YOGURT

(*Yaourti*)

Yogurt is delicious as a sauce with meat and pilaff, as a
[s]ad dressing, or as a sweet—strawberry-, pineapple-, or
[va]nilla-flavored, or with sugar or a little honey. (See Yogurt
[D]ressings.)

  Fresh whole milk or half-and-half
  Cultured yogurt

Heat milk to 180° F. To each quart add 1 to 2 tablespoons
[cu]ltured yogurt (obtainable in most health food stores), or
[re]gular yogurt saved from a previous batch diluted with a
[litt]le warm milk. Pour into a clay crock, cover with a blanket
[or] terry cloth and set in any warm place (105° F.) for three
[or] four hours until firm like custard. When set, store in re-
[fri]gerator.

Half-and-half may be substituted for whole milk if a richer
[yo]gurt is desired.

SKIM MILK YOGURT

(*Arab Style*)

Water
Powdered skim milk
Yogurt culture

This recipe is a little easier to follow and more desirable i
someone is on a diet.

Heat water to a rolling boil, then let stand until you ca
hold your little finger in it and count to ten. Add powdere
skimmed milk—⅔ cup to each quart of water, and ½ cup c
any other yogurt culture (obtainable in most health foo
stores).

Place in clay or porcelain jar or crock and wrap wit
blanket or terry cloth. Let stand for three hours in a moder
ately warm room, then refrigerate.

ITALIAN WINE VINEGAR

(*Red*)

Pour one gallon of your favorite red wine into a large glas
porcelain or crock container, add one handful of uncooke
spaghetti, broken into small pieces and one handful of u
cooked rice, cover with a cheese cloth and let set in preferab
a cool, dark place for 60 days. Then pour off amount neede
for table use or table cruets. Replenish your supply by refillin
the container containing the original vinegar mother with th
same amount of red wine that was taken out.

Friends of mine have been using the same vinegar moth
for 20 years.

ITALIAN WHITE WINE VINEGAR

Use your favorite white wine and follow the above directions.

CHILI VINEGAR

4   Tablespoons chili peppers, finely chopped
2   Cloves garlic, finely chopped
1   Sprig parsley, finely chopped
1   Sprig chervil, finely chopped
1   Quart vinegar
4   Tablespoons brown sugar

Place the pepper, garlic, parsley and chervil in a large glass jar.
Heat the vinegar and pour over the ingredients in glass jar.
Add the brown sugar and stir until dissolved.
Place the jar in the sun and shake daily.
Allow to stand for three weeks, then strain off and bottle for future use.

HERB VINEGAR

2   Tablespoons of any of following herbs: tarragon, burnet, chili peppers, mint, parsley, chervil and chives, all chopped very fine
1   Quart white wine vinegar

Add 2 tablespoons of any of the above finely chopped herbs or a combination of herbs to the white wine vinegar and allow to steep in a crock or porcelain container for two or three weeks, then strain off.
A crushed clove of garlic will add zest to the vinegar.

FINES HERBES VINEGAR—I

2 Cups of tarragon vinegar
2 Tablespoons of garden cress, chopped fine
2 Tablespoons of sweet marjoram, chopped fine
2 Cloves garlic, chopped fine
4 Small green capsicums (peppercorns), chopped fine
2 Shallots, chopped fine

Mix the ingredients in a pint fruit jar, cover closely, and set in the sun; after two weeks strain, pass through filter paper and store in tightly corked bottles.

FINES HERBES VINEGAR—II

1 Pint tarragon vinegar
2 Tablespoons seeds of garden cress, bruised or crushed
2 Tablespoons celery seeds, crushed
2 Tablespoons parsley seeds, crushed
4 Capsicums, chopped fine
2 Cloves garlic, chopped fine

Mix the ingredients in a pint fruit jar, cover closely and set in the sun; after two weeks strain, pass through filter paper and store in tightly corked bottles.

NASTURTIUM VINEGAR

Fill a quart jar loosely with nasturtium blossoms fully blown; add a shallot and one-third clove of garlic, both finely chopped, half a red pepper, and cold cider vinegar to fill the jar; cover closely and set aside for two months. Dissolve a teaspoon of salt in the vinegar, then strain and filter.

TARRAGON VINEGAR—I

Fill a fruit jar with fresh tarragon leaves or shoots, putting them in loosely; add the thin yellow paring of half a lemon with two or three cloves, and fill the jar with white wine or cider vinegar. Screw down the cover tightly, and allow the jar to stand in the sun two weeks; strain the vinegar through a cloth, pressing out the liquid from the leaves; then pass through filter paper, and bottle for future use.

TARRAGON VINEGAR—II

2 Tablespoons tarragon leaves, finely chopped
2 Tablespoons tarragon stems, finely chopped
1 Shallot, finely chopped
1 Tablespoon chives, finely chopped
2 Tablespoons brown sugar
1 Quart white wine

Blend together the tarragon leaves, stems, shallot, chives and brown sugar. Place in a crock or porcelain container, or large glass jar.

Heat the wine to boiling point and pour over the ingredients in container.

Allow to set for 15 days, then drain off.

Vinegar improves by allowing glass container to stand in sun and shaking it several times while herbs are marinating.

GARLIC MAYONNAISE TOAST

(*Serves* 4)
—to accompany the salad—

1   Cup mayonnaise
½   Cup parmesan cheese, grated
4   Fresh green onions, chopped fine
½   Teaspoon garlic powder
1   Loaf sour-dough French bread, cut lengthwise, then
    to crust in 1½-inch slices

Blend the mayonnaise, cheese, onions and garlic powder until smooth.

Spread thickly over the bread and place under the broiler until delicately browned.

GARLIC CHEESE TOAST

(*Serves* 4)
—to accompany the salad—

¼   Pound butter
1   Cup parmesan cheese, grated
1   Tablespoon garlic powder
    Paprika for color
1   Loaf sour-dough French bread, split down the cen-
    ter and cut into 3-inch slices

Melt butter in the top of double boiler, then blend well with cheese and garlic powder. Ladle onto each surface of sliced French bread making sure that you stir while you ladle a well-proportioned amount to cover the complete surface of each piece of sour dough French bread. If you are a Michelangelo, use a paint brush instead of a ladle.

Place pieces 4 inches below direct flame of broiler. Remove when golden-brown color begins to permeate the center of the cheese-covered surface.

Sprinkle with paprika for color or garniture and serve hot, blanketed with napkins.

INDEX

Index

〜